Karma in the Horoscope

Helen Adams Garrett

ISBN-10: 0-86690-614-2
ISBN-13: 978-0-86690-614-2

Cover Design: Jack Cipolla

Published by:
American Federation of Astrologers, Inc.
6535 S. Rural Road
Tempe AZ 85283

www.astrologers.com

Printed in the United States of America

Contents

Introduction

There are seven key areas in the interpretation of the karmic horoscope. They are:

- The karmic degree chart which reveals an additional view, some points which may have previously been overlooked.
- Saturn describes the lessons of life.
- The twenty-ninth degree may be a lesson in tolerance since it results in too much or too little.
- Retrogrades which are to be completed or repeated.
- The Nodes present the purpose of life.
- Declinations spell out karma in more detail like what and who.
- Interceptions describe the things we must earn a right to enjoy.

In short, if we are required to serve someone we do not desire to serve, that is considered payment of a karmic debt. This may simply be the result of having exercised poor judgment, either in this lifetime or a former one.

Now reverse the role. If someone is serving you, it is that person who is in the role of the karmic debtor.

To go a step further, doing good when no debt is owed is believed to relieve some karmic stress, while knowing to do good and neglecting to do so or taking advantage of someone contributes to karmic debts.

In any case, the natal chart, along with transits and progressions being intertwined with the declinations and their interpretations, adds up to a picture of one's karmic condition and can make a very interesting study.

Remember that every person in your life is represented in your chart. That is, your brothers and sisters and neighbors are described and represented by the third house, Gemini or Mercury. Gemini is not a karmic sign, but the third house and Mercury may be. If your chart shows you have a karmic debt by way of the planet Mercury, then you owe your brother, sister or neighbor. A planet other than Mercury situated in the third house and in southern declination will give more detail. For instance, Jupiter would imply that you are required to be generous toward those persons, or you may owe philosophical or spiritual obligations.

Chapter I

The Karmic Degree

Using an equal house chart with the Ascendant set for the karmic degree provides greater insight into the role of this lifetime. The karmic degree is the midpoint between the Sun and Moon. You can calculate midpoints with astrology software, or by hand.

If you do not have astrology software, you can calculate the Sun/Moon midpoint mathematically. As an example, say the Sun is at 2 Cancer 13. To this you would add the degree of the Moon (in this example, 28 Capricorn 21). The signs are numbered one through twelve, Aries through Pisces.

Formula: Sun + Moon divided by 2 equals the midpoint. There are two midpoints in a circle: the midpoint and the opposing degree.

Cancer	90°02:13	or	Sign 4	02:13
Capricorn	270°28:21		Sign 10	28:21
	360°30:34	or	Sign 14	30:34

Dividing the result by 2 gives:

	180°15:17	or	Sign 7 15:17

Note: 180° = Libra, thus 15 Libra 17, or 7 = Libra, plus 15°17′

Now put 15 Libra 17 on the Ascendant of a blank chart.

For a male, the Sun must fall in the top half of the chart. If it does not, use the opposite degree (15 Aries 17). For this example with the Sun at 2 Cancer 13 (being in the top of the chart while using 15 Libra 17 on the Ascendant), the Sun at 2 Cancer 13 would be in the ninth house when using an equal house chart.

For a female, the Moon must fall in the top half of the chart; if not, use the opposite degree. For this example it would be necessary to use the opposite degree, or 15 Aries 17, on the Ascendant. Using an equal house chart, the Moon would then fall in the tenth house.

For clarification, in the case of twins, one a male and the other a female, the male's karmic degree would be opposite that of the female's. The male's Moon will always be in the bottom half of the chart and the female's Sun will always be in the bottom half of the chart.

Once the karmic degree has been determined, use the same degree (Sun/Moon midpoint) on each house cusp to create an equal house chart; that is, the second house cusp is 15 Scorpio 17, the third house cusp is 15 Aries 17, etc. Then place planets accordingly. The female's chart would have 15 Taurus 17 on the second house cusp, Gemini would be on the third house cusp, etc. Then write your natal planets in the appropriate houses, according to sign and degree. When complete, your karmic chart will have the same information as your natal chart, but with the degree and sign of the Sun/Moon midpoint (or its opposite) on the Ascendant.

This chart will add much insight into the interpretation of the natal chart. You can use both your natal chart and your karmic chart to interpret the various karmic factors: Saturn, retrograde planets, twenty-nine degree planets and the Nodes. Compare and contrast the meaning of Saturn in the different houses of the two charts (karmic and natal), and look for more interpretation information by watching and keeping track of daily transits to this planet.

One of the real benefits of utilizing the karmic chart is its application to Ascendant interpretation. For example, to study career potential, turn the chart so the karmic degree is on the tenth house and read the chart with a focus on the second (income source), sixth (work and service) and tenth (career) houses. Similarly, to take a close look at health as applicable from the karmic horoscope, turn the chart so that the karmic degree is on the sixth house. Experiment with several charts to get the feel of the Ascendant interpretation; turn the chart one house at a time and analyze each house to obtain more details on the life of the individual.

Chapter II

Saturn

Saturn in the karmic chart shows where there are lessons to be learned. The native may not learn these lessons easily or early, but there will be evidence that the individual has been bombarded with many opportunities to do so. The lessons will sometimes be learned early in life, but this is uncommon.

As an example, a person with Saturn in the first house, especially if square the Sun, will find life's lessons in and through the father or another male. More likely than not the person was separated from the father at a very early age and had to learn early how to respond to older males or authoritative males. Another person with Saturn in Taurus or Scorpio may be one that seldom has sufficient possessions for the necessities of life indicating that the person has not yet learned to use the Saturn in Taurus energy to their advantage.

Most people will start life with difficulty in the areas represented by Saturn and will then consider further encounters to be challenged. After a while these encounters can become profitable opportunities to salvage (use) the energy beneficially.

Saturn in the Signs

Saturn in Aries is to learn self-discipline as the first lesson, or all else is impossible. Other lessons are: self-esteem gained through recognition of effort put forth; self-respect by not doing things which would be unacceptable to those respected by the individual; fulfillment of ambition through the personal effort and initiative and the desire for accomplishment; and independence by learning to work without assistance and complaint. To state it simply, when Saturn in Aries performs as it would judge someone else in terms of self-esteem, self-respect, fulfillment of ambition, and independence, the natural result is personal self-esteem. Lessons are best learned from experience, although some lessons may have been learned early in life.

Saturn in Taurus is to learn to use material possessions and to build through accumulation. Comfort is of ultimate importance to Taurus and material possessions relate to the individual's comfort zones. To be surrounded by misery would be a total loss to Taurus. Comfortable possessions include real estate, furniture, luxury automobiles, quality food, and things of beauty such as flowers and jewelry. Exposure to such material items promote an attitude of harmony and stimulate the desire to build through accumulation. This Saturn is to learn how and when to be patient and impatient. Enthusiasm is expansive and Saturn in Taurus needs to work toward slow growth rather than get rich quick schemes. Organizing what is accumulated is important to greater success and peace of mind, allowing better regulation of patience and impatience. Some lessons may have been learned early in life. Saturn in Taurus was born to be in control of a sizable portion of material values.

Saturn in Gemini is to learn to use of knowledge for purposes other than the accumulation of useless information. Learning appropriate and fruitful techniques of study is typical for one with Saturn in Gemini. Saturn in Gemini seems not to reduce the desire to learn and to know but to provide reasons for gathering information. Knowledge alone loses much of its value if it is not kept in motion, and it often finds its outlet in sales or teaching. Saturn in Gemini provides an excellent asset for vocational fulfillment once the individual has selected the proper avenue to follow. Numerous life lessons related to communication are experienced and learned through, with, or because of a brother or sister. The sibling may be older and authoritative, or the individual may have had responsibility for a younger brother or sister from an early age. Gemini is one of the signs of youth, so Saturn in Gemini usually learns life lessons early, especially those that come in the form of a sibling.

Saturn in Cancer is to learn how to bring the respect and responsibility of family into proper perspective, and to be emotionally sensitive. This individual may have been born into an overloaded household with a list of chores waiting to be taken over. Or one of the parents may be ill, missing, or irresponsible and the individual must learn to be an adult prior to puberty. But in adulthood this seems normal because it is all the native has known. There may be separations from family members which could result from karma by death or unavoidable distance because of career choices of various family members. Saturn in Cancer is to become hardened to certain uncontrollable circumstances yet remain sensitive to expressing deep feelings in times of grief, dissatisfaction, success or pleasure. Saturn in Cancer is born into the school of experience and although the individual may learn much early in life, there is a tendency to postpone many lessons. Saturn in Cancer may provide the ground for learning through making a home with a friend who becomes family if Saturn falls in the eleventh house.

Saturn in Leo is to learn that in order to be an honorable leader one must have the respect of followers. The native must also learn that one must love if love is to be returned. Saturn in Leo is to learn not to be a show-off because when attention is worthy it will be available. This individual is also to learn that there is responsibility in parenting and that parental authority is honorable when handled with love rather than the use of a crude, dictatorship type of parenting. These rules also apply to romance in the life of the individual with Saturn in Leo. There is the potential of separation between the individual and the father or of being under severe discipline. The native with Saturn in Leo may be designated as one who is destined for responsibility in leadership such as experienced by royalty or in government service. Saturn in Leo is endowed with much pride and makes an effort to please. This person may learn many lessons early in life; however, unreasonable authority may result in negative attention.

Saturn in Virgo is to learn respect for Mother Earth and the rules concerning sanitation. This includes purity of life in such things as eating of clean food, practicing safe sex, maintaining a natural unpolluted environment, and appreciating the body by getting plenty of sleep and exercise. Above all, Saturn in Virgo must serve, if for no other reason than to be personally fulfilled. Saturn in Virgo often finds solace in jobs or careers that provide a "service of love," such as in caring for the ill or transporting the infirm. It is well known that Saturn in Virgo may learn lessons through working with real estate or in agriculture. Some individuals use Saturn in Virgo by teaching the less fortunate to use body aids through therapy programs. Saturn in Virgo could translate as "use of perfection." In this light we find the "make the world right" people who are the religious messengers who tell it like it is (as they see it). To be successful they must first learn self-righteousness and the difference between inspection and criticism. Some learn important lessons early in life.

Saturn in Libra is to learn about relationships and in particular how to share and develop the art of accepting from the partner without guilt or obligation. There is a restlessness surrounding Saturn in Libra due to the knowledge that any potential partnership brings with it responsibility beyond the call of duty. The Saturn in Libra person also has an air of social adaptability, and this is the person who can associate with those of both high and low social status even though they may not themselves feel comfortable under all circumstances. It is a placement that raises people above the cultural standards into which they were born. A partner or coworker expects above-average performance from this person, but to the native, the job, instead of being done to perfection or with great purpose, must be done attractively according to personal taste. For the Saturn in Libra native, a commitment is a commitment. This person stays with a relationship until it is finished . . . karma! Attainment of harmony without sacrifice must be learned early in life.

Saturn in Scorpio is to learn through sexual experiences and events relating to joint finances such as taxes, insurance, inheritance, the partner's income and jointly owned properties. Saturn in Scorpio imposes upon the individual the responsibility to formulate a set of moral codes that will be uplifting to the soul. If this is not accomplished, the individual is in consistent trouble varying from negligible to major. Many times the quiet experience of pain relates to sexuality. This is often based upon early training, religious or philosophical pressures, or an improper violation forced in childhood. It is essential that the Saturn in Scorpio native learn the importance of territorial and possessive boundaries from both sides of the line; that is to say, no trespassing on others nor allowing others to take undue advantage. Practical spiritual training is a valuable lesson best learned early in life.

Saturn in Sagittarius is to learn truth and a philosophy of life that is beneficial to soul growth. The value of truth and honesty lessens any difficulties of life's lessons for this person. It is to learn through foreigners or distant travel or to work hard for an education. Any planet in Sagittarius commands communication on a large scale, but Saturn imposes restrictions, delays and denials. It is to great advantage for Saturn in Sagittarius to learn to speak distinctly, if only in body language. Sagittarius implies distant places while Saturn wants to settle down. Translated, this could bring the world to the doorstep of this person as opposed to traveling afar. Saturn's restrictions versus Sagittarius' freedom promotes a personal struggle. For some, Saturn in Sagittarius may restrict or deny marriage or certification since Sagittarius rules rituals and ceremonies. Saturn in Sagittarius learns much but not necessarily early in life.

Saturn in Capricorn has the responsibility to learn how to protect the reputation. These are learned through lessons that teach an awareness that capability, responsibility and dependability are the important ingredients of success. It is not mandatory that one be the president of a major corporation to be successful. The prime business of life may be that of being an exemplary parent or employee. Saturn in Capricorn may belong to someone who must live down a family reputation rather than live up to its honor, as well as major skeletons in the family closet. This individual is to learn a solid sense of responsibility and that the responsibility is extremely personal and not to be levied unjustly. Education for this person could well be classes that bring enjoyment to life, including learning hobbies. Laughter is an effective antidote for trouble, boredom, fear, and even fatigue. Saturn in Capricorn best learns through experience early in life.

Saturn in Aquarius is to learn to be free, but also that with freedom comes responsibility. This person is also to learn through friends and through sudden, unexpected happenings. Air signs are mental: Gemini gathers information, Libra negotiates information, and Aquarius creates from information. The genius of Aquarius is to create conditions that free the masses which in turn provide circumstances that encourage the individuality and independence of the native as well as the need to be a free spirit. Saturn, as the old ruler and current co-ruler of Aquarius, stabilizes Aquarius and provides the ability to focus on unique talents and potentials. The greatest lesson for Saturn in Aquarius is to learn to apply the energy of life toward humane projects. The restriction of Saturn says that freedom comes after the native earns the right to experience it. The price of freedom may be brought over from another lifetime. Some lessons of Saturn may be learned early in life, but freedom may not come until later.

Saturn in Pisces is to learn the value of a spiritual faith with a foundation of honesty and self-control. It provides an opportunity to grow up. Having Saturn, the planet of natural hard-nosed practicality, in combination with "I believe . . . even in the impossible" Pisces is a major lesson within itself. Sure, you can swim, but three miles from the ship to shore is a along way. You can learn to walk on water first. Go ahead, lie about everything; the punishment is worse than the gains. Take the drugs and drink the alcohol; you know it makes you sick. Turn it all over to the superior spirit (God), and then follow your hunches and you will be right. Your assumption is correct. Saturn in Pisces is learning to deal with potential addictions and taking the too easy way out. Amazingly, sometimes the easy way is the roughest in the long run. That's what it's all about! Lessons may be learned early in life, but not without spiritual guidance.

Saturn in the Houses

Saturn in the first house learns to take care of self, and that other people are also capable of doing anything they can do, if they allow it. The native is a student in the school of hard knocks, but learns the lessons thoroughly. They work because they like getting results. Saturn in the first is too hard on self.

Saturn in the second house does not deny material values, it simply requires that they be earned. Saturn here will make more money or earn more valuables; Saturn works for the person. This placement may be classified as stingy but the word conservative is often more appropriate.

Saturn is the third house compels one to learn beyond demand. The individual requires that the knowledge be applicable to personal needs. There may be a speech or learning deficiency in childhood. Often Saturn in the third house is indicative to some difficulty associated with a sibling; it may even be applicable to an only child who longs for a brother or sister.

Saturn in the fourth house may deny the company of one of the parents or may have a parent who is overly zealous in control of the individual during their youth. There are many attachments to the past, such as a desire to live in the family home or some other traditional home rather than in one of modern design. One with this placement may prefer to live alone.

Saturn in the fifth house may bring a child later in life or deny children altogether. Another possibility is that it may be a hardship to rear a child or children. Saturn in the fifth house may belong to someone who finds little joy and fun in life other than work. This configuration is found in the charts of professional game players such as ball games, chess, and gambling. This is one who works at play.

Saturn in the sixth house works hard for a living. This placement of Saturn may indicate that the individual has a shortage of essential body minerals, especially calcium. No need for alarm unless there is a chronic disease, fatigue or constipation. Saturn here may bring a prominence of small animals or pets with daily responsibilities. Service to ill people may be required or expected.

Saturn in the seventh house does not necessarily deny relationships but there may be much responsibility as a result of companions. It may also be that the companion is older or acts older. Saturn is the father or stern mother figure and the native may be seeking a replacement of what was missed in childhood or a continuance in adulthood. There may be a need to take care of someone else and to seriously share.

Saturn in the eighth house cautions care in the choice of partner as the native may have to support this person. It also urges caution regarding joint funds such as insurance, retirement funds, inheritance and jointly owned property. The moral codes this one chooses are usually strict and often hard to live up to.

Saturn in the ninth house points directly to the need to be careful in sporting events and in distant travel. This placement of Saturn is frequently found in charts of people who have diligently earned certification for a career. Here is one who resists "churchy" activities and rules. Ritual is boring unless you are the director of the performance or marching alone. The lesson is that one must trust in some kind of truth.

Saturn in the tenth house is exactly where it belongs. The sign it occupies may alter circumstances but in this reputable position one is destined to strive for excellence. If failure follows, the fall is catastrophic. This position is similar to the fourth house in that it often represents one of the parents who may be missing or dictatorial.

Saturn in the eleventh house is not ideal for club membership unless one has a desire to be over-burdened by responsibility for the group. This individual has a tendency to set goals too high or to fear achieving a goal. A better choice may be to follow tradition than to try for originality such as taking someone else's project and making it work.

Saturn in the twelfth house is about learning to become aware of and to accept responsibility, or it could become a source of sadness. The positive side is that any planet in the twelfth house has the potential energy of "prayer power": the ability to concentrate in a manner that can change things in a positive way.

Chapter III

Retrogrades

Retrogrades in the karmic chart represent energies of the past that were not complete, or are to be repeated in this lifetime. These energies provide an emphasis to extend or perfect a talent, or they may represent attaining additional knowledge to add to an ongoing project from a former lifetime.

The retrograde planet may represent an element of energy that was unused or abused in past lifetime(s). Opportunities are presented in this lifetime to correct this by meeting the challenge to develop that energy in a positive manner. A retrograde planet may also represent an individual from a former lifetime with whom there is karma to be resolved or who serves as a teacher to the native in the present incarnation.

Mercury: In evaluating many charts with Mercury retrograde, several avenues were found to be prominent. Mercury represents mind set, records, contracts, writing and wit. There were a high number of Mercury retrograde natives who were often married, numerous birth record errors were noted and there were a large number of successful writers of whom more than the average were noted for wit and comedy.

Mercury stays retrograde for approximately twenty-one days, meaning that anyone born with Mercury retrograde will have it resume direct motion by secondary progression by the early twenties at the latest. This is a lifetime to settle down the thinking processes and to learn to express directly and firmly.

Mercury transits the South Node every year and is retrograde at that degree every seventh year. During the annual transit there is emphasis on matters relating to the house involved. During those years when Mercury retrogrades over the Nodes there is a change concerning matters of the house involved at the time and the theme represented by the Nodes (north and south).

Venus: Venus retrograde indicates one who is less indulgent, less greedy or less abusive to a lover because these traits rarely play a role in the life of one born with Venus in retrograde. This may be a lifetime when one must learn to receive and be appreciative of what is provided. Since Venus rules the second house, it may afford the native an opportunity to earn sufficiently in order to share. Typically it a need to learn to relax. Venus should not be associated with stress, but rather with comfort. A retrograde Venus needs to learn relaxation and an appreciation of beauty. It also means the native is to learn to love and to learn the art of self-grooming.

In viewing a large number of charts with Venus retrograde it was found that it did not deny wealth or marriage, and that musical talent is sometimes linked to the native's fame. Others seemed to have above average talent in matters representative of the sign in which Venus is found. One person who enjoyed a remarkable financial win did so with transiting Moon tightly conjunct his natal retrograde Venus.

Mars: Mars retrograde is a message to consider priorities concerning energy. It affords an opportunity to learn patience and to control temper and anxieties.

After examining many charts with Mars retrograde, I concluded that the energy can take on a lesser Mars pace, perhaps awkward or careless. Some people were identified as aggressive behind the scenes, such as military officers who were not on the front lines. Another group was made up of those who organized the masses to be aggressive for their cause. There were several who were musicians who sang propaganda or were first in their style. A large percentage were incarcerated for unlawful financial gains, and another group appeared to be courageous.

Several experienced serious injury or death. James Dean (February 8, 1931, 21:09 EST, Marion, Indiana), an actor, died in 1955 in a high speed auto crash. Later, when Neptune was conjunct his Mercury, and Uranus was opposite his retrograde Mars, the United States issued a postage stamp bearing his likeness.

Jupiter: Samuel Clemens (November 30, 1835, 04:45 LMT, Florida, Missouri), better known as Mark Twain, had retrograde Jupiter in his birth chart. Jupiter rules book writing, publishing and humor. One would certainly be hard put to be as outstanding in both areas as he was in only one lifetime. A retrograde planet indicates an effort to capitalize on a handicap.

Saturn: One man (February 1, 1917, 14:39 CST) with natal Saturn retrograde in Cancer in the first house discovered through many past life readings that he was abused, and that he neglected or ignored the woman who was his mother in the most recent lifetime. In this lifetime she had control of him as his parent and he had a great dependency on her. He frequently rebelled emotionally but on any major decision he was compelled to give in to her wishes through a sense of guilty. He finally admitted to the feeling of guilt and forgave himself for his past wrongdoing, after which he came to love her and to show her respect.

Uranus: President Harry S. Truman (May 8, 1884, 14:11 CST, Lamar, Missouri) brought about peace in an unusual way. Natal Uranus was retrograde in the first house. He was not a likely candidate for the United States presidency.

Uranus retrograde relates to humanitarian interest and affords the energy to make a mark by in some way helping other people to be free. These people need to dare to be different by taking the challenge to break the mold of routine. This may have been unsuccessfully tried before.

Neptune: Agatha Christie (September 15, 1890, 04:00 LMT, Forquay, England) had Neptune retrograde in Gemini in the tenth house. She must have had much experience in both writing and fantasy in past lives. Jupiter (truth) was also retrograde. She was one of the most prolific mystery writers of all time. Her natal Neptune was conjunct her Pluto, both in Gemini. Would this imply a mysterious past in reference to death and dying (Pluto)?

Walt Disney (December 5, 1901, 00:30 CST, Chicago, Illinois) also had Neptune retrograde. Neptune rules film and art.

Helena Blavatsky (August 18, 1831, 02:17 LMT, Ekierinaslav, Russia) had Neptune retrograde. She founded the Theosophical Society, certainly a Neptunian organization, and traveled widely to teach her theories.

Another spiritual leader, one who sacrificed on a personal level, Martin Luther King, Jr. (January 15, 1929, 11:29 CST, Atlanta, Georgia), had Neptune retrograde. He evidently came back in order to deal with his dream.

Johnny Cash (February 26, 1932, 08:14 CST, Pine Bluff, Arkansas), a drug addict-alcoholic, singer and musician has Neptune retrograde. Neptune is in Virgo, the health sign. He gave up his addiction to come into his more perfect state of being.

Retrograde Neptune may be a result of gullibility in past lives. When writing the book *Understanding Retrogrades,* I found that people with retrograde Neptune were likely to be more realistic than those who have it direct.

Prizefighter Cassius Clay (Mohammad Ali, January 18, 1942, 18:30 CST, Louisville, Kentucky) allowed himself to be beaten for money. Or did he let himself be persuaded by those who looked on and never received the first blow? This is not reality; it is Neptune.

Lew Ayres (December 28, 1908, 00:15 CST, Minneapolis, Minnesota) spent much of his life researching world religions (Neptune). His searches dug into the past.

Jim Backus (February 25, 1913, 07:30 CST, Cleveland, Ohio) was the hidden face of the voice of the cartoon character Mr. Magoo.

Max Baer (February 16, 1909, 23:00 CST) is another one who let himself be beaten on for money. Is the fight real?

John Edgar Hoover (January 12, 1895, 07:00 EWT, Washington, D.C.) with Neptune retrograde at birth spent over fifty years waging campaigns against organized crime as the director of the FBI. He also operated in a clandestine and disreputable manner.

Pluto: Franklin Delano Roosevelt (January 31, 1882, 20:45 LMT, near Hyde Park, NY) had Mars and Pluto retrograde. Both planets rule muscles, some of which he lost control of due to polio. Had he abused them in lives past? Since he had the reputation of being the most powerful world leader of his time, had Pluto in past lives groomed him for the job?

Pluto rules masses of people and morality, along with muscles, and allows the native to release anger from past lives. Pluto retrograde is found in the charts of more than half of combative sports athletes, offering emotional control through competition. It seems that most religious leaders, especially evangelists, have Pluto retrograde.

Those with Pluto retrograde are in the business of transforming souls. Examples: Mohandas Gandhi (October 2, 1869, 07:33 IST, Porbandar, India), later in life known as Mahatma (spiritual/political leader); Cardinal James Gibbons (July 23, 1834, 06:00 LMT, Baltimore, Maryland), the second American to be named a cardinal by the Roman Catholic Church; Billy Graham (November 7, 1918, 15:30 EST, Charlotte, North Carolina), evangelist; and Martin Luther King (January 15, 1929, 11:29 CST, Atlanta, Georgia), minister and civil rights leader.

Retrogrades and Karma

The word karma can be paraphrased as "as we sow, so shall we reap." Retrogrades represent what has been sown and the present life represents the time in which we are to reap. A retrograde is interpreted as an opportunity to do over again something that was not done correctly in a past lifetime. It thus behooves us to do the best with the energy of retrograde planets.

A planet turning retrograde or direct by secondary progression indicates the beginning or closing of something of a karmic nature. For example, the ruler of the seventh house progressing direct may close karma with the mate, or open the way to experience karma with a mate.

Remember that karma is not always bad; it also delivers good. Karma brings that which is deserved. People who are takers seem to think karma is unjust, but it probably wouldn't be so tough if they would give more.

Now let's take a quick look at retrogrades by planet in the light of "do it right this time:"

Mercury retrograde says don't waste your brain. There is no need to be embarrassed by taking time to learn too thoroughly. Just get the message straight.

Venus retrograde says treat others with the love and respect that you would wish to receive and keep your financial debts in order. Take care of your possessions and things that belong to others. Appreciate life.

Mars retrograde says take your time to do it right but take the time to do it. Procrastination accomplishes nothing.

Jupiter retrograde says optimism (God) is a valuable ally. If the truth is told it is not necessary to remember a lie. It is more blessed to give than to receive. Do not over indulge.

Saturn retrograde says accept responsibility for yourself and abuse no one. Practice self-discipline. Make good grades in the school of life's experiences.

Uranus retrograde says you have another opportunity to be original in thought. Don't blow it. Be a friend and you will have one. Independence requires responsibility.

Neptune retrograde says reality draws the blueprints for day dreams. No "cop-outs" allowed.

Pluto retrograde says you don't build muscle by shadow-boxing. Unite for the cause of good rather than destruction.

Chapter IV

Declinations

Have you ever noticed how the Sun's rays come in through different angles or different windows in summer and in winter? In the northern hemisphere the Sun shines more toward the south in winter and more toward the north in summer.

We speak of the south being warmer and so it is strange to say that when the Sun is north it is summer. In winter, the Sun is south of the equator and those in the northern hemisphere want to be south to be nearer the direct rays, which are warmer.

The Tropic of Cancer at 23°27′ north of the equator marks the northernmost direct rays of the Sun. This occurs about June 22 each year when Sun enters Cancer. The Tropic of Capricorn at 23°27′ south of the equator marks the southernmost direct rays of the Sun. This occurs about December 22 each year when Sun enters Capricorn. The reason for this is that the Earth is tilted 23°27′ on its axis.

The change of direction of the declination of the Sun is marked by the summer solstice and the winter solstice. At the time the Sun enters Cancer, or the first day of summer, the Sun is at its most extreme point northward—23°27′ north by declination. When the Sun enters Capricorn on the first day of winter, Sun is at its most extreme point southward—23°27′ south by declination.

When the Sun enters 0 Aries on the first day of spring, declination direction crosses the 0 south degree to the 0 north degree by declination. When the Sun enters 0 Libra on the first day of autumn, declination direction crosses the 0 north degree to the 0 south degree by declination.

Maximum northern and southern declination of the planets varies. As might be expected, Pluto and Neptune do not follow as closely to the rule as do the others. The reason is their great distance from Earth and their elongated orbital path. The maximum degree of northern declination of all except Pluto and Neptune will be near 0 Cancer in Cancer or late Gemini. The maximum degree of southern declination of all except Pluto and Neptune will be near 0 Capricorn by longitude in Capricorn or late Sagittarius.

For accurate degrees of declination, always consult an ephemeris or use a computer calculation program.

For karmic readings, it is not totally accurate to read the planets or declination interpretations using the longitudinal placement, but it is acceptable for most points. The Sun is the standard for declination rules. Some important points to remember:

1. When the Sun enters 0 Aries, it crosses the equator going north and at that same time enters the zero degree of northern declination.

2. When the Sun enters 0 Cancer, it is at the summer solstice and as far north as it (the Sun) ever goes, 23°27′ plus a few seconds.

3. When the Sun enters 0 Libra, it crosses the equator going south and at that same time enters the zero degree of southern declination.

4. When the Sun enters 0 Capricorn, it is at the Winter solstice and as far south as it (the Sun) ever goes, 23°27′ plus a few seconds.

Out of Bounds

Planets beyond 23°27′ either north or south hold more than expected power for development and can raise the native beyond what the remainder of the chart may indicate in that particular area of life. These planets are designated as out of bounds (OOB). Planets that are OOB will be found not many degrees from 0 Cancer or 0 Capricorn. The position depends upon the planet and where the Sun is at the time.

Babe Ruth's OOB Moon gave him appeal to children. Mercury out of bounds provides skills in communicating. Venus adds to money-making wisdom. Mars enhances energy, and Jupiter is exceptionally verbal. Saturn may go from the lowest job to top executive. Uranus is unbelievably inventive. Neptune may be a terrific musician, and Pluto gives muscular development. These dimensions set out the ecliptic path, and any planet which goes beyond the maximum, at the solstices, is considered to be OOB:

- Mercury is known to go as far as twenty-six degrees north or south.
- Moon, Venus and Mars are found to go as far as twenty-eight degrees. They reach the maximum in cycles. The Moon will go OOB two or three times a month for half an eclipse cycle (nine and a half years) then not go OOB at all for another half cycle. Think what this means to progressions. One born in an OOB cycle will have a progressed OOB Moon every few years, whereas one born in a non-OOB cycle will never have the Moon progress out of bounds.
- Jupiter was OOB four or five times in the twentieth century and only for a short time.
- Saturn and Neptune have not been out of bounds in recent times.

- Uranus was OOB at three different periods during the twentieth century for about four years each time.
- Pluto is a different story all together. All the other planets are OOB very near the solstices; that is, late in Gemini through early to mid Cancer and late Sagittarius to early to mid Capricorn. But this is not the case with Pluto! It was OOB from February 1938 to May 1953—not every day, but a rough estimate would total an equivalent of about ten years. This phenomenon occurred between 28 Cancer and 21 Leo, which is almost a whole sign from the summer solstice at 0 Cancer. As far as is known, no other planet goes OOB in Leo.

In general, any planet located from 0 Aries to 29 Virgo, or in the first six signs of the zodiac, is in northern declination. Any planet in the last six signs is in southern declination. Pluto must be checked, but most others within about six degrees of 0 Aries or six degrees of 0 Libra can be estimated by north or south by reading the longitudinal degree. Remember, this is both above and below the zero points. For example, in August 1944, Neptune was already two degrees into Libra but was still at zero in northern declination. Check the ephemeris for planets between 8 Aries and 22 Pisces and between 8 Libra and 22 Virgo.

Planets located in southern declination are those we are karmically working through in this lifetime. If we have continued hardships relating to these planets, we're not dealing wisely with that energy. The planets in northern declination indicate where we have power and talents to deal with that karma and to build good credits for another lifetime.

As for interpreting the meaning of these karmic points, use the same keywords as for any other chart reading. A Moon in Aquarius is a Moon in Aquarius. Some of the key words are emotions, home, women and family for the Moon, and friends, organizations, hopes and wishes, and goals for Aquarius. What house does it occupying? Put it altogether and find how, where and with whom you are to work karmically.

Declinations can be progressed. Go back and check the progressions of your Moon by declination and you will find that there was emphasis in related areas when the Moon by declination progressed from northern to southern or from southern to northern declination; in other words, at crossover.

Declinations vs. Parallels

A parallel is when two planets are in the same degree by declination and within fifteen minutes orb, both in southern or northern declination. By some authorities, a full degree orb may be allowed.

A contraparallel is when there are two planets in the same degree and within fifteen minutes orb, one in southern declination and the other in northern declination. By some authorities, a full degree orb may be allowed.

The parallel is interpreted much as you would the conjunction in longitude, and the contraparallel is interpreted much as you would the opposition in longitude.

The degree of declination is a position of the planet and the parallel and the contraparallel are aspects from one planet to one or more other planets. Two planets that are parallel may not be in the same sign.

In this study we are not so much concerned with the aspect as with the position. Any planet located in southern declination of your birth chart represents karma that you deal with in this life based on something, someone or some attitude carried over from a past life.

A planet located in northern declination is not something to be worked out in this lifetime; it is a planet of help. If there are inclinations toward neglect or abuse, then one may build karma to work out in a future life. These aspects would more nearly be trines where we are prone to let things happen, or in irritating squares from Mars or Pluto and in northern declination.

Paying Karmic Debts and Collecting Credits

In general, planets located by longitude in the last six signs are in southern declination and are your karmic indicators. As stated previously, karma may also be collected, such as from love, service or material values, or from someone who took advantage of you in a past life. Here again we look to trines and sextiles and some conjunctions. The trines and sextiles may reach from the planet in southern declination to one in northern declination, meaning you may have to take part in the culmination of the settlement. Or, if both planets are in northern declination, you may get it a gift that comes in the form of something you may wonder whether you deserve. You may have earned it in a former life.

Progressed planets near the zero degree changing from north to south or south to north by declination can signify a change of attitude. Remembering that planets in southern declination are planets representing karma allows us to realize that it is a warning to be very careful how we use the energy of the planet in the early years or we may find ourselves paying a karmic debt in the later years. On the other hand, if the progression is from south to north we may find more pleasure and less pressure from that area of life after the progression has been accomplished.

It is interesting to note that when the Moon by progression crosses over the north-south or south-north zero degree by declination, changes are made related to home or family. Crossover planets will be found by longitude not many degrees from 0 Aries and 0 Libra.

Be sure you distinguish the difference between degrees by declination and degrees by longitude. Declination is by north and south, and longitude is by sign. Although we can approximate the extreme declination and zero declination by the sign location, for accuracy always consult an ephemeris or computer printout.

The Crossover and Extremes of Sun and Moon

If the Sun or Moon by declination will by progression cross over the zero degree from south to north or from north to south, the person can realize the change from one attitude to another.

A Pisces Sun, for example, will be in southern declination at birth. That person knows when he or she gets brave or fearless for the first time because the nature of Pisces is to wait for assistance and encouragement; but when the Sun progresses into Aries and crosses over into northern declination, the veil has been lifted and confidence is born. Some karma at this point may have been paid off.

A Virgo Sun is in northern declination at birth and will within thirty years progress into Libra and southern declination. That person, who was born with a willingness to serve, may one year find that it is easier with a coworker and that it is the coworker with whom karma suddenly appears.

Any planet can be in this area of the chart and progress over the zero degree from north to south (Virgo to Libra) or from south to north (Pisces to Aries), but these are the only points where this can occur.

The Moon will progress around the entire chart and through all twelve signs every twenty-eight years. You can learn in more detail how to interpret declinations by going back to your own chart and finding the years when your progressed Moon made a crossover by progression. Just go to the ephemeris for the day of birth and see when the Moon progressed from Virgo into Libra and from Pisces into Aries.

Karma of Planets and Signs by Declination

Sun in northern declination:

Aries: Ego expressed independently and energetically.

Taurus: Ego expressed through possessions and valuables.

Gemini: Ego expressed through knowledge.

Cancer: Ego expressed through family and homeland.

Leo: Ego expressed through leadership.

Virgo: Ego expressed through service and health.

Collecting debts, Sun in northern declination:

Aries: By not having interfered with others in the past is now left alone.

Taurus: Love given in the past is now received.

Gemini: Used knowledge to teach in the past is now allowed to learn.

Cancer: Having nurtured in the past now holds loved ones close.

Leo: Leads now, having learned to follow in the past.

Virgo: Heals now, having served in the past or experienced illness.

The above will reverse next time if negative now.

Sun in southern declination:

Libra: Ego expressed through partnership.

Scorpio: Ego expressed through morals.

Sagittarius: Ego expressed through generosity.

Capricorn: Ego expressed through humility.

Aquarius: Ego expressed through unconditional love.

Pisces: Ego expressed through compassion.

The above will reverse next time if negative now.

Collecting debts, Sun in southern declination:

Libra: Learns peace and Justice through partnerships; receives love.

Scorpio: Learns to adjust through transformation; gains inner confidence.

Sagittarius: Learns to give as well as receive; experiences truth.

Capricorn: Learns to stoop and conquer; gains honor.

Aquarius: Learns not to discriminate; envoys friendships.

Pisces: Learns to stand under pressure; gains stability.

Get the above right, or do it over.

Paying debts:

Sun in northern declination alone will not deserve a debt, but afflictions to the Sun can encourage us to put karma on the layaway plan to be paid at a later date or lifetime.

Aries: Pays through consideration.

Taurus: Pays by giving.

Gemini: Pays through sharing knowledge.

Cancer: Pays by caring.

Leo: Pays by releasing control.

Virgo: Pays through tolerance.

Libra: Pays through independence.

Scorpio: Pays by forgiving.

Sagittarius: Pays through dependability.

Capricorn: Pays through responsibility.

Aquarius: Pays through commitment.

Pisces: Pays through empathy.

Moon

Many people are born into a family or create a family through which karma can be resolved, painful as it may be. For some, the Moon is a particular woman, most likely the mother. One theory is that a summation of emotional actions and reactions is life's record of the soul, directly responsible to the Moon.

Aries: Impulsiveness in personal interest builds karma; consideration settles debts.

Taurus: Selfishness builds karma; help-fulness settles debts.

Gemini: Gossip builds karma; kind words settle debts.

Cancer: Controlling through moods builds karma; maturity settles debts.

18

Leo: Possessiveness builds karma; trust settles debts.

Virgo: Condemnation builds karma; constructive assistance settles debts.

Libra: Harsh disagreements build karma; negotiations settle debts.

Scorpio: Promiscuity builds karma; true devotion settles debts.

Sagittarius: Disrespect for other's property builds karma; honesty settles debts

Capricorn: Authoritative abuse builds karma; respect of self and others settles debts.

Aquarius: Abusing creative ability builds karma; humane services settle debts.

Pisces: Waste of life builds karma; love of life settles debts.

Mercury

Mercury's location describes one's communication style, whether used positively or negatively. Communication is how we get our message across. It may be a language, written or spoken. It may be body language, a motion of the hand, a nod of the head, a pucker or pout of the lips, a raised eyebrow or lowering of the eyelids.

Mass communication can be applause, cheering at a ball game, shoving at a sale, bowing in prayer, shedding a tear or opening the eyes in wonderment. Public communication may be visual or audible and take the form of a parade, a political speech, an advertisement or a billboard.

Bookkeeping and business records are a form of communication. We have silence, a thought of the conscious mind or a lift into the higher consciousness for meditation. One-way communication is radio or TV and two-way is telephone, texting, email, and social media. Thought transference may be psychic impressions.

Who is to say what a cosmic-karmic debt of a particular Mercury is? Example:

Someone does not speak or hear, was born deaf-mute. Are we to assume that person is paying a karmic debt? The person may not object to the condition while someone else may be very disturbed by it. Who then has the karma? A woman attending one of my workshops pointed out that Mercury had progressed retrograde about seventeen years prior and asked how it would affect her when Mercury progressed direct in four years. I did not know anything about her and commented that her manner of communicating had changed seventeen years previously and that in four more years she would likely resume or return to some previous mannerisms. She became very excited and pleasure bathed her face as she explained her happiness that if she lost her hearing again she would not have to listen to all the unnecessary conversation that had been put upon her after she gained her hearing. She said, "I can enjoy silence again." Was it her karma or someone else's ? Remembering that karma is "we reap what we sow," it is not difficult to know if Mercury is producing a good crop.

Mercury in southern declination in good aspect to:

Sun: Can grant communicative authority. Abusing the authority can bring unhappiness.

Moon: May provide good relationships with siblings; taking advantage could bring unhappiness later.

Venus: May present opportunity for love and/or money but abuse could bring unhappiness.

Mars: May win at sports and get publicized but abuse may lead to injury.

Jupiter: May gain through legal affairs. Illegal actions could cost freedom.

Saturn: Grants organizational ability. Cheating could result in downfall.

Uranus: May be overly independent through originality. Destructive genius is hazardous.

Neptune: May be an exceptional artist. Could become an unproductive dreamer.

Pluto: Has power of persuasion. Could become tyrannical.

What about northern declination? Southern declination has experience from the past. It is easy to fall back into old habits. Northern declination is not credited with karmic debt.

Freedom of choice is how we act and react. It is up to us to control those choices. If we believe in the theory of reincarnation and karma, we support the philosophy that what is sown will be reaped.

Venus

There is a saying that what we do not use, we lose. This application of Venus, wherever found in the chart, will produce good karma. Venus is the planet of love, beauty and wealth.

Venus in northern declination relates more to personal, romantic and family contacts. Venus in southern declination relates more to universal freedom and success.

Venus in northern declination:

Aries: First love. One love.

Taurus: Love me tender. Love me long.

Gemini: Love that makes sense.

Cancer: Love of family and home.

Leo: In love with love.

Virgo: Sterilized love (clean money).

Venus in southern declination:

Libra: Home companion; karma is search for soul mate.

Scorpio: Sensual; karma is spiritual.

Sagittarius: Free soul; karma is know to do good.

Capricorn: Honor bound by character; karma is balance love and money.

Aquarius: Rather have a friend than a lover; karma is friends can make strange bedfellows.

Pisces: Ideal love on a pedestal; karma is pay the price for good love.

Love is like a cold germ. Both can be given away as much as you like to whomever you wish. And you have just as much left as when you started, maybe more.

Perhaps the karmic lesson is in the judgment of distribution. Life gets complicated for anyone who loves someone who does not return that love.

Sex and love are not one and the same. Both go more smoothly when one understands the difference.

A negative reaction to Venus can result in greed or gluttony and the karmic seeds may produce thorns. A positive reaction to a southern declination Venus can settle karmic debts.

Consider the chart of Clark Gable. His Venus is parallel Saturn and Uranus, all in southern declination. Neptune in northern declination is contraparallel Venus. He had many (Uranus) sad (Saturn) love affairs and a deep love experience with Carole Lombard, who died fairly young. Though his personal love was lacking, he was the idol of millions he never knew. Neptune put him in films where he was seen and known but did not come into personal contact with those who admired him. Neptune in a multiple sign says more than one put him on a pedestal.

The Moon at 17N declination granted power with women. The planets of sexual expression, Pluto and Mars, are in degrees of talent in northern declination. His karma to be resolved is Venus in southern declination.

Mars

Impulsive action is shown by Mars. Anger and accidental injuries are related to Mars. Mars tends to be careless. The positive energy is to stop before acting. Example karmic energy listed below illustrates that actions can promote karma in the next lifetime.

Mars in northern declination:

Aries: Personal injury and ambition.

Taurus: Careless with possessions and money.

Gemini: Reckless communication.

Cancer: Petty emotions.

Leo: Careless love.

Virgo: Overwork, undue criticism.

Mars in southern declination:

Libra: Open enemies; karmic lesson is harmony.

Scorpio: Temptation to be immoral; karmic lesson is there is a higher power.

Sagittarius: The runaway; karmic lesson is practice what you preach.

Capricorn: there's a job to do; karmic lesson is do it.

Aquarius: live and let live; karmic lesson is love thyself.

Pisces: Self-destruction; karmic lesson is you're okay, keep faith.

Planets in northern declination do not leave one free to take advantage of others because any abuse now will have to be repaid later. Those who let someone else do all the chores have easy aspects. Taking too much for granted may bring extra work and responsibility at a later date.

Most people have a scar on the body represented by the location of natal Mars. Mars in Aries or the first house or conjunct the Sun yields a scar on the head or face. Mars in Taurus, in the second house or conjunct the Sun yields a scar on the neck. Most of these scars come fairly early in life and are the result of someone's error.

Anxiety can be the root of injury, anger, carelessness or discordant expression of emotions. Mars also supplies the energy we use to get out of the way of oncoming trains, mad bulls or falling rocks. It is the application of the energy that is important.

Mars is aggressive and energizes in satisfying desires, and thus is the instigator of sexual expression. This sexual energy is a physical release and can be either constructive or destructive. Constructive brings happiness and destructive brings karma.

Jupiter

Jupiter is our philosophy of life, which is the basis of our generosity and application of knowledge and wisdom. Knowledge is what we know, and wisdom is what we do with it. Knowledge is finding out the stove is hot, and wisdom is not getting burned the second time. Jupiter at its beat learns that whatever is sent out comes back. "I shot an arrow into the air and it came to earth I knew not where." But it did come back to earth.

A non-caring Jupiter may fire at random and hurt someone he or she loves. A caring Jupiter wisely checks direction for a target. Expanding wisdom through generosity, love and a warm far-sighted attitude can assure one of excellent returns. Your arrows will land safely. The secret? Loving optimism.

When things come easily, beware that karma is not being built. Jupiter is big, whichever way it tips the balance.

Jupiter in northern declination has some potential dangers that build karma:

Aries: A lot of I.

Taurus: Great accumulator, stomach overload.

Gemini: All talk; watch promises.

Cancer: Judge: "Do you have children?" Witness: "Not any I know of."

Leo: "My kingdom for a horse." Bad trade.

Virgo: Virus, virus, virus.

Jupiter in southern declination yields clues for healing karmic debts:

Libra: Two is a partnership.

Scorpio: Takes two to . . . .

Sagittarius: Gets donations.

Capricorn: Responsible payoffs.

Aquarius: Free to be free.

Pisces: Well, who cares? We do.

Because Jupiter is fun and pleasure, it is not plain to the individual that Jupiter is the seat of the problem. A run through the houses may give insight.

Jupiter in the houses:

    First: Careless, irresponsible.

    Second: Too generous.

    Third: Much talk, little do.

    Fourth: Castle too large.

    Fifth: All play, no work.

    Sixth: Eats too much.

    Seventh: Too many partners.

    Eighth: Is given too much.

    Ninth: Needs to settle down.

    Tenth: Undeserved honors.

    Eleventh: Unreasonable goals.

    Twelfth: Deceptive.

Saturn

Wherever Saturn is found in the chart there are restrictions, delays and lessons to be learned. If in southern declination, they could relate to some neglect in the past.

Saturn represents experiences, which means that those events or perceptions will be at hand more than once or for an extended time.

Experience of trial and perfection comes by elimination of error. Saturn serves us very well when experiences are evaluated and mistakes acknowledged.

Saturn in northern declination signals where the lesson is to be learned:

Aries: Impatient Aries needs to get it right the first time so it can be marked off the list.

Taurus: Taurus can do anything Taurus wants to do. Saturn may require more challenge and patience.

Gemini: Learning comes easily for Gemini, but the impossible takes a bit of concentration.

Cancer: Some cakes are made with artificial sugar. It's not always "home sweet home."

Leo: Nobody wants to follow if you don't take time to know where you are going.

Virgo: Serve or be served. Take up thy bed and walk. It's dangerous to throw stones from a glass house.

Saturn in southern declination:

Libra: Your required decision, partner or not. Adjust accordingly.

Scorpio: Scorpio revolutionizes while Saturn tries to stay the same. Whatever one believes about the Supreme Being does not make it so, but you will need to settle on something. Sagittarius: You may find a need to cut the homebound strings. Try it. You might like it, whatever it is.

Capricorn: Experience is no good unless you use it. Have faith. Live!

Aquarius: Want to be a hermit? Won't work for you. You'd eventually have to go to a store to buy materials to build a better mouse trap.

Pisces: Swim in another guy's fish pond instead of walking in another Indian's moccasins.

Uranus

Uranus represents freedom wherever it is found in the chart. It holds an urgency that is of great fearless force.

Uranus in northern declination:

Aries: Refuse to be dependent or dictated to.

Taurus: Can become independently wealthy.

Gemini: Word is not to be questioned; will speak opinions.

Cancer: Wants to be free not to be like the family.

Leo: Demands freedom in romantic affairs.

Virgo: Needs to be free to analyze; the computer kids.

Uranus in southern declination:

Libra: Marital freedom, short term relationships.

Scorpio: Moral freedom, has no fear, hard to discipline.

Sagittarius: Philosophical and religious freedom; last cycle established new churches.

Capricorn: Independent and corporate business, prefers irresponsibility.

Aquarius: Freedom to defend a friend, fights for freedom.

Pisces: Psychic and religious; the last ones paved the roads out of the church and opened the new age doors.

Neptune and Pluto

Neptune and Pluto are so far from the Sun and Earth that the pattern of 0 Aries and 0 Libra are not applicable to the zero degree of northern/southern declination.

Noting that major changes occur when a planet is crossing the zero degree from northern to southern or vice-versa, observe historical events which coincide with the declinations of Neptune and Pluto at their crossing point and at the maximum. Example: Both Pluto and Neptune were around zero during the Civil War. Pluto was at northern maximum and Neptune was at zero 1944-45, WW II. Could this account for the statement that "a child born during war years will fight a war"?

Everyone born between 1864 and 1987 had Pluto in northern declination, giving talent to those born prior to 1900 and from 1972 to 1987, and giving power to those born between 1900 and 1972. Pluto crossed over into southern (karma) declination in December 1987.

Neptune has been in southern declination since 1944, perhaps helping to explain why so many have had to deal in some way with drug (both addictive and medical) problems and religion. Changes in psychic sciences could be added to that also.

Certainly more insight could be had by considering the house of Neptune of anyone born since 1944 with Neptune karmic.

Neptune in southern declination by house:

First: Mysticism.

Second: Financial.

Third: Mystic mind.

Fourth: Home belongs to someone else.

Fifth: Unknown or unclaimed children.

Sixth: Undiagnosed disease.

Seventh: Mysterious partner.

Eighth: Sexual mysteries, financial loss, visits from spirits.

Ninth: Mystic philosophy.

Tenth: Mystical business.

Eleventh: Mysterious friends and goals.

Twelfth: Hidden enemies and fears.

Conclusion

In any interpretation the keywords should always be honored. Mars is Mars anywhere and it takes on the flavor of the sign. This is true whether the chart is natal, progressed, horary, weather or a study in declinations.

For declinations, add to the above the idea that northern declinations and the first six signs are applicable to present and future and southern declinations and the last six signs are applicable to the present and past.

The best way to learn any new interpretation technique is to take the ephemeris and go back to past experiences. Apply the technique to the astrological circumstances and study your own chart because you know your own experiences.

When the majority of planets from Jupiter through Pluto are in southern declination, winters in the northern hemisphere are colder. When the majority are in northern declination the winter will be milder. If we apply this same technique to people the interpretation would be that people with the majority of outer planets in southern declination are more impersonal and colder in personality than a person with a majority of the outer planets in northern declination.

This agrees with the suggestion that the personal attitude is related to the first six signs and the other person's attitude is related to the last six signs. The first six signs are more private in relationships, while the last six are geared toward groups and are therefore less personal.

Karma does not always say we get what we deserve. Let us use the illustration of buying and selling in the material world. If you have cash for something you want it is immediately available to you. This can compare with northern declination planets being wisely used. If cash is not ready but you have sufficient credit, you must pay interest. This compares to wise use of southern declination or paying a penalty for unwise acts from northern declination. Wanting without being able to pay can apply to incomplete learning from the past (southern) or experience to prepare for the future (northern).

Use your own examples and soon interpretation of declinations will make sense to you. Please use the positive approach. It is not all bad to be without funds to purchase something you want because you can learn how to make the best of situations.

Love promotes forgiveness to clear past debts and love breeds success and paves the way for good karma in the future.

If we live each day as if it were our last, karma takes care of itself.

Chapter V

Interceptions

An interception occurs when an entire sign is located completely within a house. A few degrees of the end of the previous sign are on the beginning cusp of the house and a few degrees of the beginning of the following sign are on the closing cusp of the house, with an entire sign in between. When one sign is intercepted the sign opposing it will also be intercepted. There is less likelihood of interceptions near the equator and a greater degree of likelihood of interceptions nearer the north or south polar regions. There can be two or more pairs of signs intercepted in a chart, and at the higher latitudes as many as ten signs can be intercepted.

When there are interceptions the same sign is on two (or more) house cusps. These are called duplicated house signs. For example, a chart with Gemini intercepted in the ninth house has 29 Taurus 48 on the ninth house cusp and 3 Cancer 06 on the tenth house cusp. The ninth house thus has twelve minutes of Taurus and three degrees and six minutes of Cancer to add to the thirty degrees of Gemini, for a total of more than thirty-three degrees in the ninth house.

Since Gemini is intercepted in the ninth, Sagittarius must also be intercepted in the third with 29 Scorpio 48 on the third house cusp and 3 Capricorn 06 on the fourth. We then we find 2 Libra 43 on the Ascendant and 29 Libra 15 on the second house cusp with the first house holding only 26°32'. This means that the seventh house also contains only 26°32' and the sign of Aries is on both the seventh and eighth house cusps.

As for interpretation, the interception is translated as being "shut out," "in a closet," or "in a drawer." To illustrate, houses three and nine (thought, communication, education, higher mind, etc.) are not readily available. There is hesitancy in open expression in many areas even though the individual is talkative. Full education was delayed. The person went back to college after age forty, although she has always been a gatherer of information.

The interceptions open up once the native has earned the right to unlock the door. It is mainly the rulers of the duplicated signs on the cusps that are the keys that open the door. In the example given the woman went to college after her husband died. Venus occupies her seventh house and rules the ninth of higher education. Pluto (death) rules the third and is in the tenth (career).

Now let's look at the first and seventh houses with the lesser degrees. This individual frequently says, "I'm not sure who I am." She has spent her life doing what was expected of her, and expressing less of herself (first house). Over the many years she was married her husband's work kept him away from home more than he was at home. Seventh house companionship was less than normal because of his absence. Now that karma is gone and passed, her next two marriages will no doubt be more full-time; she has three planets in the seventh house and unless the first husband was an extremely complex man satisfying all her needs, she will doubtless have two more marriages.

Let's say that Cancer and Capricorn are the duplicated signs on dual houses and that Cancer rules the Ascendant and the second house, and Capricorn rules the seventh and the eighth houses. It has been found that in such a case the two planets ruling those houses were afflicted. The only chart I found with the two ruling planets not severely afflicted was an individual with the money houses covered by the entire sign and having the second/third and eighth/ninth ruled by the planets. This woman has been given abundance all of her life and has had plush political jobs despite little education and her very good mind. She is also miserable and never had a job she liked. People with the ruling planets afflicted seem to manage more effectively, although with difficulty, and are happy and responsible.

The charts I found with the sixth/seventh and first/twelfth houses duplicated by rulership are people who are conscientious about service and work and appear to have it all together but have a deep insecurity.

Same signs on first/second and seventh/eighth get caught up in giving and receiving for partnership's sake.

Same signs on second/third and eighth/ninth have financial ups and downs that find their way through it by rationalizing or spiritualizing.

Same signs on third/fourth and the ninth/tenth have difficulty in attaining formal education but are not short on knowledge.

Same signs on fourth/fifth and tenth/eleventh are frequently in home and business upheavals but seek pleasure through children, creativity, friends and social groups.

Same signs on fifth/sixth and eleventh/twelfth devote much time and service to children or hobbies and fun at the price of social discord, or spend more time with friends than on personal creativity and children.

The houses encased by the two sets of duplicated signs seem to be short-circuited, and this means too much demand and not enough energy. Any aspect to the ruler gets a double draw because it rules two houses. The planets that rule the duplicated signs are the keys to opening the interceptions.

Chapter VI

The Moon's Nodes

The Nodes in the karmic chart represent the purpose in life. The South Node is always exactly opposite the North Node. These two points represent the ecliptic crossing of the pathway of the Sun and the Moon. The Nodes are always very near the degree of the last solar and lunar eclipses nearest the birth date.

Many astrologers ignore the Nodes. I find them exceptionally explanatory in viewing life's motives, moods and purposes. The North Node is said to be like a small Jupiter and the South Node is said to be like a small Saturn. Since Saturn represents past experiences the South Node is said to be placed according to the past experiences of former lifetimes and that this is a rut we are to climb out of and the that we are to go toward our North Node where areas of optimism (Jupiter) for this life are located.

The North Node indicates a point of blessings, while the South Node indicates responsibilities or challenges. That is about as far as some care to apply the Nodes. The late Isabel Hickey taught that the South Node, being the past, represents what we are to evolve from, and the North Node is what we are to develop into. This seed of thought grows into one phase of the study of karma.

Older texts refer to the North Node as the Dragon's Head and the South Node as the Dragon's Tail. The head certainly is appropriate to symbolize where one is headed, and the tail, being on the elimination end of the body, represents release.

Why would the Nodes have such an impact? They represent the road paved by eclipses. One who attaches any importance to eclipses should have no difficulty in seeing the relativity of the Nodes as they interact with planets. Many notable figures have been born concurrent with eclipses, and eclipses are frequently followed by major historical events.

The pathway of eclipses shows where major changes have taken place and where life's focus has been. If this pathway shows the past, then certainly we can use it to predict the future because hindsight is far more accurate than foresight. The eclipse pathway is known as the Nodal Path or Ecliptic Path. When you were born, the placement of the Nodes was very near the location of the last solar eclipse before your birth. This is your prenatal eclipse. (See *Your Prenatal Eclipse* by Rose Lineman for more information.)

We spend our lives doing those things described by the signs in which the Nodes are found in the birth chart. As a long-time practicing professional astrologer, I have observed that some people seem to be stuck in the negativity of the old indulgences of the South Node and have made only minimal strides toward the North Node. Others seem to have developed positively in the North Node from early childhood.

We seem to come into life with habits or acceptances of circumstances that hinder or block advancement. The South Node represents areas in which we need to apply experience and wisdom to launch new adventures in the present. Dwelling in the totality of the South Node in later life can become depressing. The application of astrological interpretations can help to open doors to the talents and capabilities of the North Node. The South Node is like a cup: ☋. It holds the past until we turn it upside down and go into the shelter of the North Node: ☊. It looks like a shelter.

Consideration of the South Node in the signs describes what has been brought from the past; its house placement lends more detail to the present life.

Example: A man with the South Node in Cancer wanted since childhood to be an FBI investigator. He had Mars, Uranus and Sun in the eighth house and was exceptional in private matters. But he was stuck in his South Node because he accepted that, as he said, "Mother didn't want me to move away." He lived within walking distance of her until her death just six months prior to his own. The Cancer South Node was in his first house of what he wanted to do. He did everything he wanted to do as long as it met with his mother's approval until his second Saturn return. Shortly thereafter, he married a woman whose Sun was exactly conjunct his Node and who had Mars (do something even if it's wrong!) conjunct his Saturn (the past). They moved into the home with the mother to take care of her and she happily released him to his new wife, his North Node in his seventh house.

The Nodes being opposite each other imply that a balance is to be reached. The South Node is were the energy has been in lifetimes past and is sometimes too comfortable. We prefer to remain in this rut but it is through the North Node that values come and we need to make special effort to follow that route.

Since the South Node represents past experiences, we build on them.

South Node is in Aries: value through partnerships.

South Node is in Taurus: value through inheritance or joint financial ventures.

South Node is in Gemini: value through specialized education.

South Node is in Cancer: value through business experiences.

South Node is in Leo: value through organizational and group activity.

South Node is in Virgo: value through institutions or compassion,

South Node is in Libra: value through developing self-esteem,

South Node is in Scorpio: value through possessions.

South Node is in Sagittarius: value through communication and knowledge.

South Node is in Capricorn: value through the home, family or women.

South Node is in Aquarius: value through a love relationship or self esteem.

South Node is in Pisces: value through service.

Nodes in the Signs

The Nodes relate to energy that is the purpose of life, and the North Node shows where the benefits are. When reading the below descriptions, think also of Aries as the first house, Taurus as the second, Gemini as the third, etc.

Aries (or First House) North Node: The purpose of life is to become independent, ambitious, self-sufficient, and positively aggressive while having a full appreciation of the importance of others, whether the contacts are personal or with the general public. The result will be self-confidence, leadership and success in favorable ways that bring happiness.

There is a need to rise above being overly dependent and to bring charm from the Libra South Node in order to become worthy of being at the head of the line in business, pleasure and daily life. The balance to be gained is a cooperative state between self-reliance and dependency.

Taurus (or Second House)/North Node: The purpose of life is to become practical in material values and sensible enough in physical activity to use the body sufficiently to absorb food consumed. There is a deep need to be of service to others which may be the means of attaining an income.

The ego should rise above greed and resentment and bring natural survivorship and spiritual depth from the South Node of Scorpio. One needs to become relaxed and temperate in all issues of life, whether in material resources, personal indulgences, or spiritual values.

The balance to be gained is between the spiritual and physical elements. Physical includes not only material possessions but sexual practices.

Gemini (or Third House)/North Node: The purpose of life is to make use of communication to gather knowledge and information and to teach from a basic level, all of which can be applied to improvement for the individual. There is a benefit in accomplishing an inner peace through mental development to overcome nervousness.

Ego is to rise above levels of gossip and communication errors and to draw upon the ability to be optimistic, which is the natural ability of the South Node of Sagittarius.

The balance is between gaining worthwhile knowledge and wisely applying it.

Cancer (or Fourth House)/North Node: The purpose of life is to find someone, some thing or a project to nurture. The instinct to care for others is strong and should be developed either as personal satisfaction or as a vocation. There is a need to build toward security and to express sincere emotions.

Ego is to rise above being bossy and controlling and to use the ability of the South Node in Capricorn to organize time to allow for protecting family, family-like groups or individuals.

The balance is between emotional security and material security, which should result in spiritual security.

Leo (or Fifth House)/North Node: The purpose of life is to find love. It cannot be fulfilled until there is a dismissal of self-centeredness. There is a need to become appreciative of personal talents and potentials in order to elevate self-esteem and to love and respect self in a way worthy of a self-confidence that can overcome jealousy. There is a strong need for attention which must be deserved, not demanded.

There is a need to rise above a negative "I know" attitude from the Aquarius South Node energy and to become a leader with loving sensitivity who maintains the Aquarius sociability.

The balance is between one-on-one relationships and contact with the masses.

Virgo (or Sixth House)/North Node: The purpose of life is service in a manner that assists others to better themselves in some way through health, finances (as "the money counter") or sanitation, and in any avenue that will lead people to perfect the world around them. There is a built-in desire to correct things, and sometimes there is an effort to satisfy that desire by marrying someone who is unhealthy or a failure of sorts.

There is a need to rise above the negative energy of the Pisces South Node that can create excuses for turning away from responsibility. People with the North Node in Virgo can sometimes reach a higher road by becoming involved in services related to spiritual growth.

The balance is between serving and being served.

Libra (or Seventh House)/North Node: The purpose of life is to learn to live in harmony with others and to become decisive even in small matters. Learning to negotiate and to compromise are of great importance. Making an effort to cooperate provides more potential for success. Accomplishing the art of forgiveness makes life more pleasant. One with this placement of the North Node usually has to learn to accept gifts or gratuities without denying the pleasure of the giver to give.

There is a need to rise above total aloneness, as supplied by the energy of the South Node in Aries, and to accept the presence and assistance of others. It is important to understand that others want to help, too.

The balance is between aloneness and togetherness, recognizing that one is never completely alone. This, of course, can have its advantages and disadvantages.

Scorpio (or Eighth House)/North Node: The purpose of life is to intensify spiritual faith and to evolve from concentration on material values. It is beneficial to be involved in interests relating to survival, whether of the mind, body or spirit. They ultimately overlap. Overcoming resentments and learning to release and let go are of great significance to this placement of the

North Node. It can be advantageous to make practical use of material and earthly properties and possessions, as provided by the positive side of the Taurus South Node. There is a need to rise above vengeance and to become spiritually discriminating in use of the power of destruction.

Balance is between spiritual issues and material needs which keep body and soul together while on earth's sojourn.

Sagittarius (or Ninth House)/North Node: The purpose of life is to teach a code of honesty in all issues. It is important to learn to face adversity in order to establish strength. Knowledge supplies basic truth to the Gemini South Node, while the Sagittarius North Node needs to remember to get more facts in order to specialize. Life's lack of understanding for this placement comes from not wanting to begin with the basics.

There is need to rise above running away. It is natural to run away, but challenges that promote soul growth require facing facts. It is also natural to run in circles; in time, there it is again. We either come back to it or it follows us. That's karma.

Balance is between gaining knowledge and applying knowledge.

Capricorn (or Tenth House)/North Node: The purpose of life is to learn self-discipline and to accept responsibility, performing accordingly. There is a desire to be frugal. Spiritual laws say, "Not at someone else's expense." Salvaging is a masterful art, if acquired. Maintaining an emotional balance is important. Experiencing some of the emotionalism of the Cancer South Node has value if it is not an indulgence. Lack of emotional expression appears inhuman and cold.

There is a need to rise above the pettiness of the Cancer South Node and to accept the challenge of organizing personal life and to nurture family in a mature and positive way.

Balance is between emotions and responsibility.

Aquarius (or Eleventh House)/North Node: The purpose of life is to feel accepted without losing freedom. There is a need to experience commitment without the possessive negative energy of the South Node in Leo. It is important to learn to release original thoughts and ideas in a practical manner that can bring recognition as well as self-esteem. This can provide a touch of genius that can result in success.

There is a need to rise above conceit and false pride. Many tend to live far above their means. Universal love and community interest will supply personal satisfaction provided the positions of leadership are not too heavy.

Balance is between freedom and commitment. This placement should enjoy involvement through group activity.

Pisces (or Twelfth House)/North Node: The purpose of life is to find the niche for happiness where sacrifice can become pleasure instead of martyrdom. It is important to participate in the removal of unwanted conditions in order to bring all things to a better state of being. This placement stoops to conquer when helping someone of lesser circumstances.

There is a need to rise above the garbage of life and not be involved in destructive criticism of the South Node of Virgo. It is important to remember that even the smallest fish in the sea in some small way will feed the world.

Balance to maintain sanity and good health is somewhere between idealism and perfection.

South Node Conjunct Planets

Did you ever think about a habit following from one lifetime to another? Or, even if you don't accept the theory of reincarnation, consider how things flow from childhood into adulthood. One woman said her family never allowed anyone to put visitors' coats on a bed. She thought it was a superstition, and called her mother from a group meeting to ask about it. Her mother said, "That started many years ago when you kids were little. We had bedbugs and didn't want our guests to get them in their coats." The woman had been married several years, had her own home and was relieved to no longer have to provide a closet just for guests' coats.

The South Node is rather like that. We may not know why we are stuck in its energy, or even that we are stuck. Somewhere along the way we may drop a portion of the past but hesitate to move fully into the North Node. On the first Saturn return I dropped allergies, but it was not until the second Saturn return that I dropped poor health.

A planet conjunct the South Node identifies luggage from the past. Not every chart has a planet conjunct the South Node, but transits will make the conjunction, and anyone more than age twenty-eight has experienced the Moon or a planet progressed to that point. I would venture to say that by progression the conjunction deals with something of the present lifetime that needs to be adjusted. It may seem strange that the South Node represents the past. Karma is cause and effect. You don't open a wrapped gift until you become aware that it is yours. Since the South Node is like Saturn, and also the past, when the subconscious accepts responsibility for the past, it then becomes open, as karma.

One thing is very important to remember when you study karma. It is not necessarily "bad." There are a lot of people who didn't enjoy school but were later very glad they did. Karma is the school of experiences.

South Node Conjunct Sun: The Sun rules Leo—royalty. The individual has been in a high position in some or many past times. It is time now to become just one of the crowd and be humble. In the present the Sun might encounter individuals from the past and might try to control them; however, this may be their time to be controlled. Being born stuck in self-involvement can be a tough lesson.

South Node Conjunct Moon: The soul remembers emotions from the past. The Moon rules family, the general public and women in particular. Best favors will not come forth from these people. Who is left? Friends, neighbors and business associates. This one may be separated from family in the present, and may be stuck in emotional frustration from birth until healed. One with the South Node conjunct the Moon will probably break family ties and may not do well in public office.

South Node Conjunct Mercury: This one talks and thinks much but has difficulty accomplishing the end, or may have a brother and/or sister who was a close contact in a past life. A best friend may be someone who is a brother or sister now or was one in a past life. He or she probably experiences nervous disorders until they advance to the North Node. There is a need to focus on the more important things first, one of which is mental relaxation. One has to avoid becoming stuck in mountains of paperwork or on the phone.

South Node Conjunct Venus: Beautiful (handsome) in past lifetimes and is spoiled by it in this life. Gets too much attention from people for whom there is no personal interest and, needless to say, not enough from the desired sources. This one had ample material possessions in the past and now has financial difficulty until working into the North Node. This is an individual who is stuck in leisure and a desire for luxuries.

South Node Conjunct Mars: This conjunction attracts conflict. It is a warrior from the past or one who demands much from others who are ready to settle the score this time. This placement might also indicate a quick temper with slow physical movements, and there might be an abundance of ambition but difficulty staying on track. Mars is stuck in unnecessary anxieties and anger. Solution: Work toward the North Node.

South Node Conjunct Jupiter: There was much freedom in the past. Jupiter represents laws, whether of the land, family and household, school or the workplace. The individual had difficulty in abiding by restrictions and rules, and there is a lack of understanding of this. Somewhere along the way a penalty must be paid. When that lesson is learned, the level of spirituality will automatically be elevated.

South Node Conjunct Saturn: Usually works harder than necessary to earn everything because of a sense of responsibility. Held authoritative positions in the past, so the person may be pushy in the present. Goals are not easily reached because there is a subconscious dread of taking charge. May be stuck in old habits until an attitude of optimism and a lessening of the need to control is reached through function toward the North Node.

South Node Conjunct Uranus: The free spirit does not want to meet with a schedule, but the rest of the world does not always comply. Individuals might be stuck in having their own way to the point that it could repel potential friendships. This one has unique and original ideas, but in this lifetime has a need to develop more stability of the kind that will be described by the North Node in its placement.

South Node Conjunct Neptune: Confusion results because of uncertainty due to confinement or interference in the past. Visions of idealism might not always produce ideal consequences. There is an inclination toward romantic or poetic dreams of success, and the native is prone to addictions of various kinds. This one often has outstanding musical talent. Goals become more realistic after working into the North Node.

South Node Conjunct Pluto: This individual may be found in historical records if one knows where to look. Pluto implies a powerful past whose strength may have been physical, mental or spiritual and was not necessarily favorable (or unfavorable), but it was strong. The native is probably impatient, dealing in power struggles in the present. Now it is time to relax and build spiritually.

North Node Conjunct Planets

It matters not whether one knows or has ever heard of astrology because there is an instinct to make an effort to fulfill the purpose of life. North Node is the present, or present lifetime, and a planet conjunct (within a five-degree orb) shows where we can expect assistance in accomplishing this purpose.

North Node Conjunct Sun: There are benefits in association with people of prominence and authority. Know your own worth and talents and be proud of who you are.

North Node Conjunct Moon: Sharing emotional issues with family and the general public is beneficial. This is a good placement for real estate, public relations, politics or the food or service industry.

North Node Conjunct Mercury: This individual benefits through knowledge, paperwork, close relatives and communication skills. There is much talent in the use of the hands and in writing ability.

North Node Conjunct Venus: Venus benefits from beauty products, clothing, social activities or dealing with money or objects of comfort. The native may very well find a lover from a past life. Life is easier after leaving the South Node.

North Node Conjunct Mars: This native benefits from physical activities, such as sports or construction work, or could benefit from something related to the eyes. Success may come through the use of knives or guns, such as surgery, the military or police work. Verbally, Mars might be expressed in the ability to debate, and is persuasive.

North Node Conjunct Jupiter: Here we have the teacher, traveler, author or lecturer who is likely to be in frequent or constant contact with foreign countries or people. This one may benefit through distant travel or a philosophical life as a counselor or religious leader.

North Node Conjunct Saturn: This disciplinarian is capable of handling responsibility and authority, and enthusiastically accepts challenges after leaving the South Node. The native learns to live by tradition and profits from past experiences.

North Node Conjunct Uranus: There is a talent for originality and an ability to work with and through social activities. Friends assist in many ways, especially as depicted by the house of this conjunction.

North Node Conjunct Neptune: This gives a talent for the arts, which may be through the written or spoken word in addition to form, color or music. It may point toward politics, and there is an influential air of mystery. One positive approach is in the promotion of idealism.

North Node Conjunct Pluto: This one has great power of persuasion and might deal in the unknown—psychic, investigations, exploration, or sciences.

Nodes in the Houses

The placement of the Nodes by sign tells us our life purpose, and the location by house gives a closer look. We are born stuck in the South Node because we have had one or more lifetimes in that mode. We may have been so busy that we neglected family, or we could have been poor or

hungry, and now it is our turn to have more. We could have come from royalty and now must learn to be the servant. A past frail body may now have the opportunity to be an athlete. Now, in the present, we are to learn from the opposing experiences.

Interestingly, it seems easier to convert the past energy of the South Node to the present need of the North Node when we are in a close relationship with someone: a partner, a family member, or perhaps a friend or coworker who has the Nodes the reverse of ours. In such an instance we help each other without realizing it. These people will have age differences in alternate increments of nine years; i.e., nine, twenty-seven, forty-five, etc. years older or younger. For example, if the South Node indicates a tendency to alcohol, a parent who is twenty-seven years older or a grandparent who is forty-five years older might be the complimentary force that sends us on the road to sobriety without ever having had the first sip. But be aware! Alcoholism may not be the only vice the South Node offers.

Knowledge of the sign of the opposing house should easily point you to where you might still be stuck in the South Node. It might not be as simple as changing only one negative habit. Most of us engage in several transformations in a lifetime.

Karma comes in various forms. We might have unfinished business or incomplete relationships, or we might be coping with situations or circumstances from lives past. We might have health problems from abuse of some kind. Whether we believe things or not is not important. What is important is that when we study the Nodes in the natal chart, we are able to find good information to help us improve our lives . . . now.

Keep in mind that what we do, even without knowledge of astrology, is to try to get away from the lesser advantages of the energy of the South Node and work toward the fulfillment of the North Node. Here are some affirmations:

North Node in First/South Node in Seventh

Aries First/Libra Seventh: "I've spent enough lifetimes stepping aside for others and it only got me to the end of the line. This time I'm first."

Taurus First/Scorpio Seventh: "No sex tonight. I'm going to bed to relax after I eat. Tlomorrow there is money to be made! Now, let's snuggle."

Gemini First/Sagittarius Seventh: "Oh, no, you go around the world touring temples and watching ball games. I'm doing everything on the telephone."

Cancer First/Capricorn Seventh: "It's your boss and your business. I'm taking the kids and spending the evening with Mom and Dad and my family."

Leo First/Aquarius Seventh: "I would love some prime time alone with you. After all, I am the most important person in your life."

Virgo First/Pisces Seventh: "I'll stop at the doctor's on my way to the office and see you after you finish house cleaning and shopping."

Libra First/Aries Seventh: "Thank you. I would be delighted to have your help. I had wondered how I would manage alone."

Scorpio First/Taurus Seventh: "There must be a solution that will put us in control. I will research until we have the answer."

Sagittarius First/Gemini Seventh: "Specialized information is needed; we may employ the largest and most reputable firm in the country."

Capricorn First/Cancer Seventh: "I have an executive meeting. Call the service station and make an appointment to have my car oiled and lubricated."

Aquarius First/Leo Seventh: "I'm not sure just yet, and won't know until about an hour before starting time. (Private thought: I don't know those people and I may get a better offer from friends.)"

Pisces First/Virgo Seventh: "We are doing our shopping and going fishing. Somebody is always picking on me."

Purpose: Be who you are supposed to be. Have the courage to let go of people and habits that are detrimental. Learn to say no.

North Node in Second/South Node in Eighth

Aries Second/Libra Eighth: "I take care of my money and you take care of my things. Thank you."

Taurus Second/Scorpio Eighth: "What is mine is mine and what is thine is mine, if you give it to me."

Gemini Second/Sagittarius Eighth: "Most of my gains come from heirloom trading or from sales."

Cancer Second/Capricorn Eighth: "I'm keeping in touch with my family and home, where my bread is buttered."

Leo Second/Aquarius Eighth: "You get all my love in exchange for security."

Virgo Second/Pisces Eighth: "I keep a close accounting of my possessions."

Libra Second/Aries Eighth: "We absolutely must have a joint bank account."

Scorpio Second/Taurus Eighth: "It is to my advantage to be private about what I own."

Sagittarius Second/Gemini Eighth: "I believe in the law of giving. What goes out, comes back two-fold."

Capricorn Second/Cancer Eighth: "It makes more sense to have my money work for me than to work too hard for my money."

Aquarius Second/Leo Eighth: "I'll take whatever from wherever it comes, provided there are no strings attached."

Pisces Second/Virgo Eighth: "If I am nice and friendly, someone will always take care of me."

Purpose: Balance material values with spiritual values.

North Node in Third/South Node in Ninth

Aries Third/Libra Ninth: "I have a right to think as I am and to speak as I think."

Taurus Third/Scorpio Ninth: "I will think it over and let you hear from me after I investigate."

Gemini Third/Sagittarius Ninth: "Well, yes, I have a couple of thoughts on the subject. Now I know. . . ."

Cancer Third/Capricorn Ninth: "I have a good track record as to knowing what the public wants."

Leo Third/Aquarius Ninth: "Both you and I know that I know whatever you want to know."

Virgo Third/Pisces Ninth: "I may appear emotional but I can usually handle a crisis."

Libra Third/Aries Ninth: "Have you got any ideas I could borrow? What are your thoughts?"

Scorpio Third/Taurus Ninth: "I must find the error and correct it so we can keep the records straight."

Sagittarius Third/Gemini Ninth: "We gather ALL the facts before we can make a proper decision."

Capricorn Third/Cancer Ninth: "I retain any and all information until it proves to have no value."

Aquarius Third/Leo Ninth: "You would be surprised at what I think and know."

Pisces Third/Virgo Ninth: "You think I am reserved but could I ever write a smear!"

Purpose: Get back to basics and apply knowledge on a daily level.

North Node in Fourth/South in Tenth

Aries Fourth/Libra Tenth: "Home and family are my self esteem and I must put them first."

Taurus Fourth/Scorpio Tenth: "I must build and own a home where I find comfort and peace."

Gemini Fourth/Sagittarius Tenth: "Keeping in touch with my family is of utmost importance."

Cancer Fourth/Capricorn Tenth: "I am my family's shield. My goal is to protect them and our home."

Leo Fourth/Aquarius Tenth: "My home is my castle and my family is my royal court."

Virgo Fourth/Pisces Tenth: "The health of my family is important. Our home must be sanitary."

Libra Fourth/Aries Tenth: "Home sweet home is where I find happiness and love."

Scorpio Fourth/Taurus Tenth: "Money is not everything. Morals are forever."

Sagittarius Fourth/Gemini Tenth: "It is my obligation to teach my family what they need to know."

Capricorn Fourth/Cancer Tenth: "I am responsible for the necessities of my home and family."

Aquarius Fourth/ Leo Tenth: "Family members are my true friends. I have individuality at home."

Pisces Fourth/Virgo Tenth: "My best foot should be behind the scenes in my home with my family."

Purpose: Remember the roots of heritage and be and bare a better stock.

North Node in Fifth/South Node in Eleventh

Aries Fifth/Libra Eleventh: "My inner self strives to be honest in the elevation of my self esteem."

Taurus Fifth/Scorpio Eleventh: "I want to be loved for who I am rather than what I have."

Gemini Fifth/Sagittarius Eleventh: "Just love me for my mind first; the body follows."

Cancer Fifth/Capricorn Eleventh: "Though I may appear to be untouched, I feel very deeply."

Leo Fifth/Aquarius Eleventh: "I need one-on-one relationships from birth; each is special in its own way."

Virgo Fifth/Pisces Eleventh: "When I work, I work when I play, I play, though work is more satisfying."

Libra Fifth/Aries Eleventh: "Hey, somebody, any body, just don't leave me alone for long."

Scorpio Fifth/Taurus Eleventh: "What I really need is someone to care for and about."

Sagittarius Fifth/Gemini Eleventh: "For my ego I must do things on a very large scale."

Capricorn Fifth/Cancer Eleventh: "My success comes from my joy of production. I love my work."

Aquarius Fifth/Leo Eleventh: "Friend/lover? Lover/friend? What's the difference? I love 'em all."

Pisces Fifth/Virgo Eleventh: "The most precious moments in life: quiet, private times."

Purpose: To learn to love and know self by developing ego and self-esteem. Then love happens. Creativity and children can be sources of happiness.

North Node in Sixth/South Node in Twelfth

Aries Sixth/Libra Twelfth: "I am personalty responsible for conditions of my work and health."

Taurus Sixth/Scorpio Twelfth: "I recognize the value of stability in my work and health."

Gemini Sixth/Sagittarius Twelfth: "I employ rational thinking in addition to practicality."

Cancer Sixth/ Capricorn Twelfth: "I must learn to honor my moods without disrupting the lives of others."

Leo Sixth/Aquarius Twelfth: "I do not impress anyone when I destroy my health being a martyr."

Virgo Sixth/Pisces Twelfth: "If I want things done my way, I must do them myself without complaint."

Libra Sixth/Aries Twelfth: "Companionship is a necessary part of my work and good health."

Scorpio Sixth/Taurus Twelfth: "To be happy and healthy, I must learn to work smart and steady."

Sagittarius Sixth/Gemini Twelfth: "I can not be all things to all people. I must be selective."

Capricorn Sixth/Cancer Twelfth: "I must learn to abide by the symptoms of stress in respect to health."

Aquarius Sixth/Leo Twelfth: "It is not necessary to experience disease to learn about it."

Pisces Sixth/Virgo Twelfth: "My faith can make me whole, but I must be aware of potential toxins."

Purpose: Use my body or lose it. Learn to care about my health. Know that work and health vibrate together.

North Node in Seventh/South Node in First

Aries Seventh/Libra First: "True cooperation is neither totally dependent nor independent."

Taurus Seventh/Scorpio First: "Partnership is a most valuable asset with rights of possession."

Gemini Seventh/Sagittarius First: "Through open communications any problem can be solved."

Cancer Seventh/Capricorn First: "Stability is not built on tears; however, feelings are bonding."

Leo Seventh/Aquarius First: "I will love you forever if you trust me and don't hold me too closely."

Virgo Seventh/Pisces First: "I know you will take care of me so long as I'm NOT perfect. Don't worry!"

Libra Seventh/Aries First: "Associates are people with whom I learn to share, and this means you."

Scorpio Seventh/Taurus First: "Please, be my best moral strength. You are mine, body and soul."

Sagittarius Seventh/Gemini First: "I chose you to help me upgrade my knowledge to wisdom."

Capricorn Seventh/Cancer First: "I am as a flowing brook. You are the dam that strengthens me."

Aquarius Seventh/Leo First: "More than anything in the world, I need a friend, and more friends."

Pisces Seventh/Virgo First: "You are my major project, the clay I mold to idealism."

Purpose: To know what I need to learn about relationships and to honor those who are my partners and coworkers.

North Node in Eighth/South Node in Second

Aries Eighth/Libra Second: "I am a taker but must also learn to give. If I love you, you may help me."

Taurus Eighth/Scorpio Second: "I seek to balance my material means with my deepest emotions."

Gemini Eighth/Sagittarius Second: "My lessons are more in truth and trust than in material values."

Cancer Eighth/Capricorn Second: "I must respect your interests as my own—no work, no pay."

Leo Eighth/Aquarius Second: "The greatest possession is love on all levels. Tough lesson?"

Virgo Eighth/Pisces Second: "I am learning personal giving. I can not give what is not mine."

Libra Eighth/Aries Second: "I am learning self-esteem and to respect my properties and yours."

Scorpio Eighth/Taurus Second: "It is important to balance my material means with my deep emotions."

Sagittarius Eighth/Gemini Second: "Things alone will not allow a happy God within self. I seek spirit."

Capricorn Eighth/Cancer Second: "Lesson: Material security promotes mental stability."

Aquarius Eighth/Leo Second: "Warning signal: Flattery is the bribery of codependency."

Pisces Eighth/Virgo Second: "My lessons in possessions equal appropriation of time and priorities."

Purpose: To find my most valuable possession and learn to develop and share it as I learn to give and receive.

North Node in Ninth/South Node in Third

Aries Ninth/Libra Third: "Education is important, even though I may have to learn it by myself."

Taurus Ninth/Scorpio Third: "I must be aware that people listen to me and be careful of what I say."

Gemini Ninth/Sagittarius Third: "Trivia is not my best goal; wisdom with teaching is my destiny."

Cancer Ninth/Capricorn Third: "Releasing resentment through forgiveness is peace of mind."

Leo Ninth/Aquarius Third: "A prophet is not known in his own land and neither am I."

Virgo Ninth/Pisces Third: "I am not to advertise myself above that which I can live up to."

Libra Ninth/Aries Third: My lesson: "t know what I know . . . but I don't know everything."

Scorpio Ninth/Taurus Third: "I must seek my spiritual truth and learn to stand by it."

Sagittarius Ninth/Gemini Third: "If I have difficulty in learning, I must go back to the basics."

Capricorn Ninth/Cancer Third: "I am to allow my faith to work for me and to discipline myself."

Aquarius Ninth/Leo Third: "Whom I know may be worth more than what I know."

Pisces Ninth/Virgo Third: "Believing may not make it so, but it draws blueprints to build by."

Purpose: To find a philosophy of life that satisfies my soul, one that is such a comfort that I can talk about it.

North Node in Tenth/South Node in Fourth

Aries Tenth/Libra Fourth: "I am to learn from my parents and not make the same mistakes."

Taurus Tenth/Scorpio Fourth: "The best things in life may be free but some things I must work for."

Gemini Tenth/Sagittarius Fourth: "I will be known as a communicator; it is desirable to stick to the facts."

Cancer Tenth/Capricorn Fourth: "I can stand on the reputation of my family, like it or not."

Leo Tenth/Aquarius Fourth: "I am endowed with leadership ability but would often prefer to follow."

Virgo Tenth/Pisces Fourth: "There may be skeletons in my closet; however, my goal is to do the best that I can."

Libra Tenth/Aries Fourth: "Together we make beautiful music or success; alone I may flounder."

Scorpio Tenth/Taurus Fourth: "In an effort to control my emotions in dignity, I may appear secretive."

Sagittarius Tenth/Gemini Fourth: "No doubt I am in the news for what I say or write."

Capricorn Tenth/Cancer Fourth: "Honor my parents, if they deserve it; then build my own life."

Aquarius Tenth/Leo Fourth: "I am shy about recognition but friendly gestures bring it anyway."

Pisces Tenth/ Virgo Fourth: "My compassion for others eventually brings me before the public."

Purpose: To openly honor who I am and to accept responsibility for the recognition that comes to me.

North Node in Eleventh/South Node in Fifth

Aries Eleventh/Libra Fifth: "If I want a friend, I must be a friend. Group activity is valuable to me."

Taurus Eleventh/Scorpio Fifth: "Social contacts are helpful to me. Friends contribute to my success."

Gemini Eleventh/Sagittarius Fifth: "I can learn many things from social activities."

Cancer Eleventh/Capricorn Fifth: "My goals are reached through friends who are family members."

Leo Eleventh/Aquarius Fifth: "I gravitate toward royal atmospheres. A lover must also be a friend."

Virgo Eleventh/Pisces Fifth: "Friends come through work or health which friends also support."

Libra Eleventh/Aries Fifth: "My partner is my special friend. My children are a reflection of me, mirrored or reversed."

Scorpio Eleventh/Taurus Fifth: "Friends are very powerful, private and can be controlling."

Sagittarius Eleventh/Gemini Fifth: "Friends tend to be impersonal frequent travelers; gregarious."

Capricorn Eleventh/Cancer Fifth: "Social contacts are almost formal and of executive nature."

Aquarius Eleventh/Leo Fifth: "Friends: Network of acquaintances who are kept at arm's length."

Pisces Eleventh/Virgo Fifth: "Social variety: artistic, mystical, inspirational, addictive."

Purpose: To dare to be different and express originality. To exchange talents with social contacts. Friends fill voids and create highlights.

North Node in Twelfth/South Node in Sixth

Aries Twelfth/Libra Sixth: "I am to learn that inspiration comes in time alone, which I enjoy."

Taurus Twelfth/Scorpio Sixth: "I can use a quiet time to plan my material ventures."

Gemini Twelfth/Sagittarius Sixth: "There is a time for everything; reading a good book is calming."

Cancer Twelfth/Capricorn Sixth: "I withdraw from protective services to others, to nurture myself."

Leo Twelfth/Aquarius Sixth: "I go to my den to lick my wounds and heal my own imperfections."

Virgo Twelfth/Pisces Sixth: "Sending spiritual healing accomplishes more than physical services."

Libra Twelfth/Aries Sixth: "What goes on behind closed doors is the height of companionship."

Scorpio Twelfth/Taurus Sixth: "There is no peace until I have forgiven transgressions."

Sagittarius Twelfth/Gemini Sixth: "There is great power in communication with the spirit."

Capricorn Twelfth/Cancer Sixth: "I may appear spontaneous but I am extremely well controlled."

Aquarius Twelfth/Leo Sixth: "Its better to be a fish in a well stocked pond than a single whale in a zoo."

Pisces Twelfth/Virgo Sixth: "Heal thyself (myself)! Believing will make it so. A challenge but I'll try."

Purpose: To turn to my strength within when I am faced with problems, and to learn to deal with issues rather than cop out.

Planets Transiting the Nodes

Karmic events occur when there is a transits of a planet over the Nodes or when an eclipse hits a planet. Pay special attention when the planets retrograde over the South Node.

Moon transiting the South Node each month brings the advantage of developing little by little the process indicated for the attainment toward the North Node.

Moon transiting the North Node brings assistance through daily routine.

Mercury transits the South Node within a few weeks of the same time each year and prompts interest or concern relative to matters of the house where the South Node is located or the houses Mercury rules.

Mercury transiting North Node provides time and mental energy for taking stock of resources, messages, correspondence and catching up on the things-to-do list.

Venus transiting the South Node roughly once a year and may bring you in contact with someone you loved or respected in the past. Now that contact may cost you. You may need to pay a debt.

Venus transiting the North Node could offer you a pleasurable meaning with someone. You could collect a debt. You may fall in love our be loved.

Mars transiting the South Node every eighteen to nineteen months may coincide with an over expenditure of money or energy or you may find that you are thrown in the company of one who tries your patience.

Mars transiting the North Node encourages you to use your energy wisely and you enjoy your activities. You may clear a karmic debt.

Jupiter transiting the South Node provides spiritual challenges. Your philosophy could be shaken,

Jupiter transiting the North Node may be a time of spiritual uplifting. You could receive gifts or take a long trip.

Saturn transiting the South Node could be a time of difficulty. This is not a time to get even, but a time to be fair. Saturn gives us what we deserve, good or not so good.

Saturn transiting the North Node brings a bonus from good past performances. If it goes by without your noticing, maybe you didn't earn much.

Uranus transiting the South Node may find you in unfriendly circumstances. You open karma, changes occur.

Uranus transiting the North Node may set you free or open your creative ability to be original. Some karma closes.

Neptune transiting the South Node could expose you to misfortunes through misconception or put you on your toes in psychic experiences.

Neptune transiting the North Node may open Your psychic awareness and bring you spiritual benefits.

Pluto transiting the South Node could escort you into an opportunity to struggle in learning through power play issues or you may be exposed to sexual unpleasantness.

Pluto transiting the North Node could release you from a long time karmic debt or open the door to exercising your personal power.

Interchart Nodal Conjunctions

What does it mean if someone else has a planet conjunct your Node?

1. The North Node has the potential to bring good things your way, and the South Node may bring something or someone you might never have wanted but through whom you can settle karmic debts and unfinished business—and may even like.

2. What is the planet? Sun, creativity; Moon, emotions; Mercury, communications; Venus, love or money; Mars, action; Jupiter, abundance, possibly too much; Saturn, the taskmaster; Uranus, society; Neptune, deception or inspiration; Pluto, power; and the Nodes, karma.

3. Which Node is conjunct which planet? For example, North Node (favorable) conjunct another's Saturn (authority): The Saturn person was an authority, perhaps a parent, employer or your slave owner in a former lifetime. This would imply that the Node person's position was satisfactory and that in this life the Saturn person will be helpful to the Node person, who will respect Saturn as an authority. South Node (not so good) conjunct another's Saturn (authority), as set out above, would find the Saturn person had not been fully pleased with the relationship in the former lifetime and presently levies strenuous superiority. The relationship is not a pleasant one until the debt is paid.

Suggestion: Give the best possible performance for as short a time as possible to settle the score. It is wise to continue to be respectful, but be sure to close the debt; otherwise, it might find its way back again in this life or, surely, in a future one. Once the debt is cleared, a good relationship can be fully enjoyed or dismissed. We certainly don't want to rack up a stack of karmic credit cards to take into the future.

The planet person feels a bond with the North Node person, who may seem indifferent. The planet person does not necessarily recognize the sense of obligation that may be haunting the South Node person.

An extremely interesting study can be done with the use of an ephemeris. Start with the outer planets, perhaps Pluto first. See if Pluto has ever made a transit over the natal North or South Node. Try to recall what happened at that time. What major change came to you through a powerful individual? Then look at Neptune, Uranus, Saturn and the other planets.

Generally you will find that the South Node brings someone into your life. Why? Because the South Node represents the karmic past, someone who comes out of the past to collect the debt owed to him or her. So you have a child whose South Node is conjunct one of your planets? No doubt it is a challenge. As surely as the South Node brings someone in, the North Node takes someone out. Karma is finished with that individual. That does not mean you will never see him or her again. It does mean your feelings change. It may be the death of someone; if so, a healing in the relationship has taken place prior to or during the passing.

4. Look at the Nodes transiting the planets.

The Sun represents children, creativity and the love force. Certainly it governs what we seek in pleasure, entertainment and self-respect.

The North Node benefits in some manner in the present by Sun, who may be an authority figure, a lover or one with whom much fun is enjoyed.

The South Node was probably a child of Sun in a past life. Some kind of payback is in order. Former physical abuse might now require care-taking. Material abuse might now require financial support. The South Node owes the Sun.

The Moon represents female figures, the mother, a woman friend or a family member. There may be a strong sense of family relationship between the two.

The North Node profits by the Moon, and a harmonious relationship is enjoyed. There is a strong emotional bond between them.

The South Node feels attraction toward the Moon due to the need to pay back a karmic debt, and also feels restricted by the Moon.

Mercury represents brothers, sisters, relatives, neighbors and younger people. There is often an overtone of brother/sister kinship.

The North Node enjoys and benefits through communication with Mercury and feels its protection and kinship.

The South Node in the relationship may be shy or nervous, thinking Mercury has more knowledge or can verbally manipulate. Mercury is probably a sibling in this or a past life.

Venus represents a lover, or at least one to whom there is or has been much devotion. There is a strong bond. It may be parent/child, brother/sister, teacher/student, friend or business associate; it can be any gender or connection.

There is a mutual devotion when the North Node is conjunct another person's Venus. Venus may give materially to the North Node or provide an opportunity for advancement, or simply pump up the North Node's ego. It may even result in what some would consider a soul mate contact. Others may not understand the connection, but feelings prevail between the two.

The South Node conjunct Venus of another brings difficulty, such as Venus getting the best bargain in a trade, Venus not paying debts to the South Node, Venus being rude or, worst of all, past life romances being paid back. The South Node may fall deeply in love while Venus totally ignores it. There may be a relationship, but one void of affection. There may be an effort to love, but somehow it does not stack up.

Mars represents energy, irritation, frustration, physical activity and anger. A Node in Mars contact could have been in war, athletic activities, industrial ventures, laying train rails or any physical action relationship.

The North Node conjunct another person's Mars most likely will promote working together or playing together in physical activity. It can be a magnetic physical attraction.

The South Node may need to be a dodger or a fast runner in the current life because chances are Mars has a punch on the nose in reserve. It is interesting to check out charts of public figures for whom you have personal feelings of conflict.

Jupiter represents teachers, philanthropists, prophets, philosophers, travelers, writers and truth.

The North Node is a terrific beneficiary when making a connection with a past life Jupiter! Jupiter is a valued counselor and advisor; the North Node seems to want exactly the information that Jupiter has available.

The South Node requires your attention! A rip-off by a Jupiter person is definitely sizable (Jupiter rules embezzlement). It might be frightening to go back into a past life or lives and find out what deserved Jupiter's justice this round.

Saturn is the taskmaster, whether in person or deed. There is positively a lesson to be learned. Saturn is father, employer, land owner, or anyone who can get away with being bossy.

The North Node conjunct another person's Saturn can allow for excellent training in business or the ways of life. Saturn contacts can be valuable in reference to any contacts dealing in solid things that come out of the earth, such as iron, copper, silver, gold, salt or stone, but not oil or water.

People usually seem to feel that the father is Saturn conjunct South Node in the present. This is probably because his mark lingers on. Saturn is the boss. Whatever treatment received is probably a deserved past debt. Best to pay and get it over.

Uranus represents friends, maybe "kooks" (I couldn't find that in five dictionaries but anyone reading this material knows one).

The North Node conjunct another person's Uranus signals an excellent friendship. Uranus might also stimulate what was otherwise dormant genius.

The South Node conjunct another person's Uranus discovers Uranus popping up in the most unusual places and doing unexpected things.

Neptune represents religious leaders, musicians, artists, hypnotists, anesthetists, psychics, liars and addicts.

Neptune can be exceptionally inspirational to the North Node even as they both go their separate ways. This inspiration can be spiritually charismatic and persuade the masses.

Neptune is just as inspirational to the South Node but in a different direction. These two will choose a more detrimental path. They may quit school together. They may shoot drugs together. They may scheme together. This is a danger sign. Pluto represents people of power. They can have the kind of power that leads a nation or the kind that turns the head of others in one small group after another.

Sexual attraction might be very strong when Pluto meets a North Node. It will vary according to the two charts because thousands are born during the time frame when the conjunction occurs. Influences other than sexual also respond to Pluto.

Pluto conjunct another person's South Node could lead the South Node into harm, or it could become a power struggle.

The Ascendant conjunct another person's North Node will assist the North Node person coincidentally if not intentionally. The Ascendant can be interpreted as another Sun.

The Ascendant conjunct another person's South Node denotes the South Node as the one who owes the debt. The Ascendant might expect interest on the centuries-old debt. It is possible for both to benefit.

There will be millions of people in a lifetime with such conjunctions who will never have contact. Those with additional energy exchange who do have contact will have an opportunity for soul growth and can be happy in the relationship if the obligation is honored by South Node and accepted by the planet.

What is the conjunction orb? The closer it is, the more certain it is to be felt. Most people do not seem to feel the energy exchange beyond five degrees.

Node/Sun: With your North Node conjunct another's Sun, that person helps you. With your South Node conjunct another's Sun, you owe that person. Treat him or her well and pay the debt. Treat the person badly and interest compounds. The Sun person was a parent, probably a father, or an authority figure in a past lifetime.

Node/Moon: With your North Node conjunct another's Moon, that person nurtures you emotionally. Your South Node conjunct his or her Moon can be frustrating to that person. The Moon person was a mother or nurturing character in a past lifetime.

Node/Mercury: With your North Node conjunct another's Mercury, you learn from that person. Your South Node conjunct his or her Mercury means you owe that person the knowledge. The South Node conjunction can be difficult in communication. A Mercury/Node contact indicates a brothers or sister in a past life.

Node/Venus: With your North Node conjunct another's Venus, the person cares about you and the contact is good. With your South Node conjunct another's Venus, you may have been lovers in a past life or abused the person in some way. You may be close now but you don't get the best treatment and will play second fiddle. You are paying a debt.

Node/Mars: With your North Node conjunct another's Mars, you get the benefit of that person's energy. You may enjoy physical activity together, including sex. With your South Node conjunct another's Mars, you are physically or mentally abused at some level. Mars/Nodes conjunctions represent combat in former lives. North Node is fighting together, and South Node is fighting against one another.

Node/Jupiter: With your North Node conjunct another's Jupiter, you desire to learn from that person. You may enjoy traveling together, and you gain through this person. With your South Node conjunct another's Jupiter, you misbehaved toward this person in a former lifetime and now you are to give to them. A good opportunity to learn forgiveness and generosity.

Node/Saturn: Your North Node conjunct another's Saturn indicates a father or authority figure you respect. You may be under this person's supervision and will learn much. If your South Node is conjunct another's Saturn, the person was your superior or parent in a past life, and you were a problem. This is your opportunity to do it right.

Node/Uranus: With your North Node conjunct another's Uranus, you are friends or at least compatible. This person inspires your creativity and originality. With your South Node conjunct another's Uranus, you are former friends and can be inspired by or follow the person. There is intrigue. Both of these conjunctions can be exciting.

Node/Neptune: With your North Node conjunct another's Neptune, there is artistic inspiration that can be psychic or spiritual. People with these conjunctions do not see each other in a true light. With your South Node conjunct another's Neptune, it may be spiritual or negative, with deception on the part of either or both. Possibly you were old drinking buddies.

Node/Pluto: With your North Node conjunct another's Pluto, there is power in the extreme. It is personal power or power in masses or groups. This conjunction allowed you to be a beneficial influence to the Pluto person. With your South Node conjunct another's Pluto, there is rebellion to some extent. You may cause the Pluto person to rebel, and there can be a power struggle between the two. One of you may have killed the other in a past life, perhaps in a war. Node/Pluto conjunctions may also promote sexual attraction, other aspects assisting, which would provide the area of interest for the power struggle (in this case, jealousy).

Node/Node: Your North Node conjunct another's North Node means that you were born near the same date as that person and have some of the same generational interests, or that there are eighteen to nineteen years (or multiple thereof) of age difference between you. You would share a purpose in this lifetime. You would not necessarily work together in that interest, just have the interest in common. Your South Node conjunct another's North Node can be mutually beneficial in that you could supplement each other in your life's purpose. Your age difference would be about nine years or nine years plus or minus a nodal cycle.

Node/Ascendant: With your North Node conjunct another's Ascendant, you benefit from the relationship as does the other person. Your South Node conjunct another's Ascendant; a strong karmic bond. You feel a sense of obligation and probably rightly so.

Chapter VII

Twenty-ninth Degree

Have you ever gone to an "all you can eat" restaurant just before closing? Most people, when informed that the food would be removed at closing, load their plates with far more food than they ordinarily would. This is the twenty-ninth degree in action: a strong need to increase the supply represented by the planet, sign and house. Approximately every two and a half years all of us can identify with this urge when the progressed Moon spends a month in the twenty-ninth degree before entering the next sign by progression.

After researching many charts, it became apparent that an appropriate phrase for the twenty-ninth degree is "can't get enough," either because none is available or because of the excessive desire. No amount seems to satisfy the want.

Karmically, the planet occupying this degree may represent unfinished business or undeveloped talents from a past lifetime, or it could represent a lifetime when that issue was denied or unattainable. As in all interpretations, there is a positive and a negative reflection. Two people with the same planet at the same degree in the same sign may develop the energy from that point in exactly the opposite manner.

The can't-get-enough attitude may be because there is absolutely no access or availability for the positive development for one person, while the other may have an abundance but is not satisfied with a normal achievement and has an insatiable desire for more and more and more, manifesting as too much or too little

If there is no twenty-nine degree planet in the natal chart, keep an eye on progressions. Progressions to this degree can be very revealing. Depending upon the speed of the planet, a progressed degree is effective from two or three months up to several years. The progressed Moon will come to the twenty-ninth degree at approximately two and a half year intervals.

Progressions to the twenty-ninth degree can be very revealing as to proper interpretations. Depending upon the speed of the planet, a progressed degree can be effective from two or three months (Moon) up to several years with the slower planets.

In doing the research for this project, a delightful woman was found with Venus at 29 Sagittarius. She openly admits that she can't get enough fun. She says she gets overly enthusiastic about anything in the way of a hobby or entertainment.

You are encouraged to look for the positive applications of interpretations. Just because something is missing does not have to mean that there is sadness relative to it. An overload is not always a burden. Learn to laugh about your twenty-ninth degree; it may become a point of pleasure to you as you major on a handicap.

All Things in the Hopper

In horary astrology we are told that when the Ascendant is past twenty-seven degrees, the chart cannot be interpreted because it is "too late." We find in a study of such charts that the degree will indicate by sign what is too late or what has been done to cause something else to be deferred or omitted.

For example, a young man asked, "Should I put the renter out?"

The twenty-ninth degree of Taurus occupied the Ascendant. He was informed that he would not be required to because it was too late, that some event had relieved him of the responsibility. During the conversation it came out that the property in question belonged to his father and he was serving only as conservator and he had, just prior to the question, stopped by the bank representing the father and consulted them about the situation.

The twenty-ninth degree says that something is about to end. Notice that the bank is an authority in the situation and the bank has been brought into the matter. Taurus rules banks and money. One of the bank officials telephoned the renter, and he promptly packed his belongings and moved out.

Another indication from Taurus and the fixed angles is that perseverance would prevail. They would remove the renter. There was enough other evidence against the renter to have taken him into legal custody and transferred to jail.

Many times a wedding chart with a twenty-nine degree Moon is found to be based on pregnancy. The family has already been established. A twenty-nine degree Moon in the wedding chart may also indicate that the home is already underway. They may have been living together for some time before or they may have bought furniture or a home.

Another example: "Will we get to take a cruise?" The Ascendant was 29 Sagittarius. The first impression was that the answer was "no." This did not hold for long because within a few hours a call was received affording the opportunity to serve as a ship astrologer. All things were in the hopper. Sagittarius rules distant travel and luck.

Twenty-nine degrees says that there is about to be a change. All of one condition is finished and an opportunity is about to open.

Aries/First House

The twenty-ninth degree of Aries relates to self. Aries can't get enough of self or for self, because personal desires are not satisfied or because of denial or interference from outside forces. The twenty-ninth degree of Aries is in the Sagittarian decan of Aries and under the Jupiterian influence, as well as Mars, which rules Aries. This is the Pisces dwad bringing confused optimism. Too much or too little.

Sun at 29 Aries: Can't get enough attention (time in the Sun) or can't get enough time to be alone. Having an inner urge to be up front or ahead of things. Other people are demanding or not cooperative. Native is learning self value.

Moon at 29 Aries: Can't get enough family or home life, or is smothered by it. This ram frequently becomes a little lamb. Read the paragraph above to better understand the emotions.

Venus at 29 Aries: Possibly due to impulsiveness, can't get enough love, and money goes fast. Or may desire to escape the fan club. Thinks choice of pleasure is the same as everybody else's. Does not understand why others do not enjoy the same things.

Mercury at 29 Aries: Can't get enough talk or education in the little things of life. No brothers or sisters, or reversed and is stuck with them. Is quick of mind, especially concerning own business or pleasure. Experiences nervous impulses.

Mars at 29 Aries: Energy shortage. Wants more action than the energy will support, or is listless. Is very ambitious or meets with much discouragement, which ultimately destroys ambition. Is learning to appropriate time and energy.\

Jupiter at 29 Aries: Can't get enough of many things, education, philosophy or travel. May be employed in some phase of law and order or may be involved in something outside of the law. Attracted to outdoor sports. Not as successful as the athlete. Has a tendency to be generous with advice and specialized information.

Saturn at 29 Aries: Can't get enough responsibility, or does not accept it. Is required to grow up too young or is forever a child. Has a desire to own a business or to be own boss. Difficulty in discipline in general or in personal habits.

Uranus: at 29 Aries: Can't get enough excitement or freedom. Friends may be a drag. May be a rebel. Has a great variety of originality, particularly concerning self and personal benefits.

Neptune at 29 Aries: Can't get enough of the real self. Difficulty in facing reality concerning self. Is learning spiritual honesty.

Pluto at 29 Aries: Can't get enough control or must take control in self defense.

Chiron at 29 Aries: In the hustle and bustle of going along inattentively one will eventually realize that the major adjustment needed, before time runs out, concerns personal issues.

North Node at 29 Aries: Needs to learn to love self but not be self-centered.

South Node at 29 Aries: Needs to learn to love others.

Taurus/Second House

Taurus is the sign of comfort, values and personal possessions, including money and income. The twenty-ninth degree is in the Capricorn decan, ruled by Saturn, having a need to combine pleasure with business. The appetite of 29 Taurus is for success through real estate and possessions. The dwad is Aries, providing a desire for personal success.

Sun at 29 Taurus: Can't get enough money and possessions because of an inability, or the desire, for more. The appetite for food may be excessive. Accumulating could be an obsession. Is learning a balance between generosity and greed.

Moon at 29 Taurus: Can't get enough home, children, family and money. Desires a home of comfort and luxury. Emotional frustrations concerning home, family and money.

Venus at 29 Taurus: Can't get enough comfort, pleasure, relaxation, love or money. Be aware of health relating to kidneys or lymph glands, or ovaries (in females). May be overly zealous in work.

Mercury at 29 Taurus: Can't get enough knowledge, clutters mind unnecessarily but can be exceptionally practical. Dwells long on the same subject.

Mars at 29 Taurus: Needs rest; plays hard. Determination to win whether at work or play. May have muscular problem. Has great earning capacity.

Jupiter at 29 Taurus: Limited enthusiasm. Learns practicality through careless efforts resulting in loss. Gives too much or too little. Has narrow escapes in financial dealings. Needs to establish strong beliefs in spiritual issues.

Saturn at 29 Taurus: Too much or too little work for wages. Has high value standards. If out of work, appears to be too dependable on others. Has positive attitude and application of abilities can be successful.

Uranus at 29 Taurus: Should pay attention to own thoughts of practical and profitable ideas. Unique talents for survival. Attracts people of wealth.

Pluto at 29 Taurus: Too much or too little financial power. Can accumulate an empire or lose all.

Chiron at 29 Taurus: It is important to place only value on material essentials but to remember that Taurus is also the loving protector needing to reap the benefits of being appreciated.

North Node at 29 Taurus: Needs to learn about material values. Is learning to be responsible for one's own self support.

South Node at 29 Taurus: Needs to learn to give and receive graciously and to establish a high moral code.

Gemini/Third House

Gemini is a mutable sign and mental. The twenty-ninth degree holds a storehouse of ideas, but needs encouragement to set them in direct motion. Being the Aquarian decan, others should remember that what might appear wild could be genius. Life could be a game. The dwad is Taurus—thoughts of fun.

Sun at 29 Gemini: Knowledgeable but uncertain. Wants to learn, but learn what? Restless toward life direction. The intellectual rolling stone. Makes effort to build ego around information.

Moon at 29 Gemini: Nervous without reason. Intellectually creative in little things. Emotionally high strung. Put upon by brothers and sisters or neighbors. Attracts public through information.

Venus at 29 Gemini: Two droplets of income. Too few or too many games to play. Likes mental exercises for pleasure. Often has two relationships going at the same time ... one may be fictitious or platonic.

Mercury at 29 Gemini: Too much or too little concentration. There is a whirlwind of knowledge and a search for a use or storage place for it. On the go again and again.

Mars at 29 Gemini: Can't get enough fighting words. Enjoys verbal wars, not necessarily angry. Mentally competitive wanting to know all first.

Jupiter at 29 Gemini: Too much or too little books or travel. Desires to be a specialist. Searches for an intellectual philosophy of life. Takes chances by expanding too much.

Saturn at 29 Gemini: Worries too much or too little. Too few or too many brothers and sisters. May do very well with foreign languages. Short term conversationalist. Takes responsibility of knowing.

Uranus at 29 Gemini: Original and creative ideas flourish but they are not readily harnessed to become reality. Can't get enough unique or interesting friends.

Neptune at 29 Gemini: Too much or too little music, languages or fiction stories. This can be a very psychic mind but may experience fears and uncertainties in early episodes,

Pluto at 29 Gemini: Too much or too little verbal power. May be very influential but does not realize the strength of the word.* When Pluto went through Gemini last some of the discoveries and inventions relating to power (Pluto) and transportation and communication were: Diesel engine, X-ray, radar and Einstein's theory of relativity of energy.

Chiron at 29 Gemini: The energy will seek knowledge in a service field of some kind; the adjustment could be toward a different focus for fulfillment.

North Node at 29 Gemini: Needs to communicate more freely in order to relieve tension. Is learning to make the most of available information.

South Node at 29 Gemini: Needs to learn mental peace. Should learn to seek new knowledge and not dwell too long on stale and obsolete material.

Cancer

Any planet at 29 Cancer will be emotional but may not be openly so, due to the influence of the Pisces decan. A planet here can result in emotional outbursts if there is no regular release of built up tension. This is the Gemini dwad enabling the individual to expound in frustration. Is surrounded by family or chooses to be separated from family.

Sun at 29 Cancer: Has too few young in the home and a struggle over authority in the family Tries to build a kingdom through home and family.

Moon at 29 Cancer: Too few or too many children. May borrow children from friends or relatives. Overly nurtures other adults. There is much absence from home for some.

Venus at 29 Cancer: Too much or too little protective affection. Is sensitive to neglect and desires more attention. Home is always open or "invitation only."

Mercury at 29 Cancer: Interested in the old family tree or could care less. Wants to be like family or totally different. Too much or too little of releasing emotions.

Mars at 29 Cancer: Can't get enough excitement in the home. Usually limits expression of anger to home and family. Is patriotic or a defector.

Jupiter at 29 Cancer: Can't get enough real estate. May desire to be free of responsibility of family and home ties. Has strong religious faith or no faith.

Saturn at 29 Cancer: Home life limited. May not have close contacts with the family. Home may need constant repair. Seeks sympathy in the home. Loss of father at early age.

Uranus at 29 Cancer: Frequently changes residence or furniture. Uses many kitchen gadgets or makes own innovations. May have difficulty finishing projects.

Neptune at 29 Cancer: Home Sweet Home may be only a dream. Searches to satisfy the ideal in home and family. Relationships may result in parent-child roles creating fictitious parenthood for substitute from childhood.

Chiron at 29 Gemini: The energy will seek knowledge in a service field of some kind the adjustment could be toward a different focus for fulfillment.

Pluto at 29 Cancer: Can't get enough self-confidence. May live very privately. Constantly correcting morals or lives as if there is no tomorrow.

Chiron at 29 Cancer: The adjustment may be to be care for family member or someone else.

North Node at 29 Cancer: Needs a family. Is learning to be emotionally expressive. Also is learning to nurture.

South Node at 29 Cancer: Needs to be weaned. Learning to share rather than to draw into self.

Leo/Fifth House

The regal sign of Leo always makes an effort to build a kingdom. The twenty-ninth degree is in the Aries decan, prompting great egoism and self-sufficiency which may repel cooperation of other people. This is the dwad of Cancer supplying great sensitivity and some insecurities.

Sun at 29 Leo: Self-confident. Draws much attention whether positive or negative. Over dramatizes; can't get enough of self. Limitation in building personal empire.

Moon at 29 Leo: The unfulfilled lover. Can't get enough romance. No children or too many children. Strong nurturing instinct. The regal parent who takes care of all. May be the caretaker of property belonging to others.

Venus at 29 Leo: Can't get enough mirrors on the wall, ceiling, etc. A craving for love and money. Has much love to give but finds it a challenge to find the ideal recipient. Some compensation comes in dealing in a business related to charm.

Mercury at 29 Leo: Talk, talk, talk, but who listens? Can't get enough talk about self. Makes reports about personal activity. Can be very dramatic.

Mars at 29 Leo: Has difficulty in finding a balance between activity and relaxation. Native is dramatic and daring. May suffer injury as a result of showing off. Too much or too little attention.

Jupiter at 29 Leo: The subject is legalities. Too much or too little honorable legal exposure. Enjoys outdoor sports or being a spectator. May major on philosophizing.

Saturn at 29 Leo: Too much or too little discipline. Is hard on self. Probably needs to be more generous. Grasping for the last straw. Should change focus when current subject becomes stressful. Heart is too small for body size, physical limitations.

Uranus at 29 Leo: Too much or too little unique entertainment. Fickle in romance and ends with hurt feelings. Will not be told what to do.

Neptune at 29 Leo: Too much or too little play. Life can get to be only a stage show. Camera buff. Too much romance and not enough love. Seeks idealism.

Pluto at 29 Leo: Limited in parenthood through which to exercise authority. Seeks opportunity for leadership Inner need to reconstruct self image.

Chiron at 29 Leo: The message may be: "To get attention be a do-gooder and leadership will follow." An adjustment toward self-esteem could be in order.

North Node at 29 Leo: Must accept leadership. Needs to work toward more confidence and accuracy.

South Node at 29 Leo: Must appreciate self more through association with other people. Needs to cultivate solid friendships. Should guard against arrogance.

Virgo/Sixth House

Virgo is the sign of service, which is required of the native according to the planet in Virgo. Or the privilege of serving is denied. The twenty-ninth degree is in the Taurus decan. Finances relate to the degree. This is the Leo dwad. Native more readily sees the faults of others than self.

Sun at 29 Virgo: Seeks to be of service, paid or volunteered. Tries to change the course of things. Makes intricate critique. May be very untidy but self-condemning in other things.

Moon at 29 Virgo: Requires much medicine or takes none. Gets intestinal upset when emotionally distressed. Housekeeping is to the extreme, clean or dirty. Fanatic concerning food.

Venus at 29 Virgo: Soap addict—Mr. or Ms. Clean or sanitation expert. Endeavors to speak correctly. Germ conscious. Too much or too little perfection.

Mercury at 29 Virgo: Corrections, corrections, corrections, is there no end? Time-is-running-out air of urgency. Learns that it is okay to make mistakes.

Mars at 29 Virgo: Looking for germs, one way or another. Can't get enough analysis. Why? Why? Why? When words fail, expresses through dirty words relating to bodily eliminations. May suffer from intestinal problems.

Jupiter at 29 Virgo: Usually scientific or medical. Too much or too little, organized or unorganized, sick or well. Philosophically analytical. May sanitize to the point of exhaustion or destruction, such as washing the paint off the walls.

Saturn at 29 Virgo: Can't get enough work because it is not available or because of being a workaholic. Works at perfection or wants no part of it. May have health problems related to diet.

Uranus at 29 Virgo: The unexpected prevents perfection or becomes perfected. Seeks to be original in health matters. Enjoys unusual food combinations.

Neptune at 29 Virgo: Can't get enough proper food. Should be on guard against build up of toxins in the system. Sets goals above normal ability. May not see imperfections. May have drug problem; drug may be medication.

Pluto at 29 Virgo: Too much or too little change. Constantly seeking something better. Excellent for researching. If mowing, cuts down everything but the house. Clears the way.

Chiron at 29 Virgo: This is the fix-it engineer. Making an effort to be happy may prove more satisfactory than changing the world. Adjust toward better health.

North Node at 29 Virgo: Must learn to serve and become health conscious.

South Node at 29 Virgo: Must learn to serve or be served, but to avoid being too dependent.

Libra/Seventh House

The sign of Libra represents partnerships and cooperation. It is also peace and culture. The twenty-ninth degree falls in the Gemini decan. This combination will stimulate restlessness in the indicated areas by house. Peace at all cost or war to-the-finish. This is the Virgo dwad. It is difficult for the individual to see self-error, or is too tough on self.

Sun at 29 Libra: The individual is not understood by others. Requires comfort. Can be a strong warrior. The author has known several who have Sun at 29 Libra and believes it to be one of the most difficult placements. Those who live in a purposeful productive way strive for approval and perfection. They get the toughest assignments at school and work. They are not allowed by society to be carefree. The negative side of this degree executes their ideal perfectionism through violence. Both are learning self-respect, self-defense, peace with others, and care of body and possessions.

Moon at 29 Libra: Emotional restlessness in the home. A desire for companionship. Is learning to select a mate. May have problems with women.

Venus at 29 Libra: Is looking for true love. Tries too hard to be cooperative. May have female health problems, kidney disorders or skin blemishes. Needs to learn to make firm decisions. The male does not understand women.

Mercury at 29 Libra: May marry many times or not at all. Too much or too little conversation. May be avid reader.

Mars at 29 Libra: Verbal warrior seeking peace. Enjoys company of others and is learning degrees of aggression when to move in and when to step aside and wait; you could call it patience or harmony.

Jupiter at 29 Libra: Seeks marriages with the most benefits. Extremely polite or of a belligerent attitude. Attracted to professions relating to law or philosophy.

Saturn at 29 Libra: Very much or very little cultural atmosphere, music, clothing, jewelry, art, etc. Is learning through relationships not to be possessive nor to allow abuse.

Uranus at 29 Libra: Too few or too many friends. Associates with unique people. Relationships form and break quickly and unexpectedly.

Neptune at 29 Libra: Graceful and charming or awkward and withdrawn. Promotes involvement in the arts. Is sometimes in a fog concerning values in attachments to others.

Pluto at 29 Libra: Cannot form a relationship or has one after another. May have no respect for others in relationships. May be abusive or abused. Experiences power struggles.

Chiron at 29 Libra: This points to adjustment in relationships. It is not a good idea to cash out without checking out both parties. The need for adjustment may be personal, if it is your chart.

North Node at 29 Libra: Must learn justice to self, as well as to others. Is learning to share and to accept.

South Node at 29 Libra: Must learn to love others in order to love self. Is learning to balance dependence and independence.

Scorpio/Eighth House

Scorpio rules the physical desires and any planet in Scorpio will tint the physical needs. Scorpio is also spiritual. Since the twenty-ninth degree is in the Cancer decan the soul requires that degree to answer to the individuals moral codes. This is the dwad of Libra urging the individual to involve others in expressing self.

Sun at 29 Scorpio: Is a long time finding self. Has a struggle within concerning personal desire versus the moral issues. Behavior tends to be impeccable or immoral.

Moon at 29 Scorpio: Sensuous. Too much or too little emotional pleasure. An inner desire to remove the sorrows of the world. May have an intense dislike for women.

Venus at 29 Scorpio: Too much or too little giving or receiving. May fail to get a fair share when an inheritance is divided. May try to buy spirituality or honors from the cosmos.

Mercury at 29 Scorpio: Surrounded by secrets. Keeps all or tells all but people keep pouring them on. Excellent investigator, but may not want to know.

Mars at 29 Scorpio: Very physical. Muscular development or weakness of muscles. One who can rebuild from an illness. Practices controlled action.

Jupiter at 29 Scorpio: Struggles between rituals and morals. Too much or too little psychological or religious knowledge. A secret desire to be morally correct.

Saturn at 29 Scorpio: Experiences exposure of primacies. Has endurance which may run out just before the finish but determination will allow recovery.

Uranus at 29 Scorpio: Too few or too many intimate friends. Has potential for great originality. Interesting view of life and death.

Neptune at 29 Scorpio: Could relate to some kind of cop out. Constantly seeking a more comfortable life style. Has psychic ability . . . neglect of or search for spiritual truth. Can be very resourceful.*

Pluto at 29 Scorpio: Urgency to change many things because of the subconscious awareness coming from Pluto in its own psychic sign, Scorpio; knows that Pluto energy in the sign of Sagittarius will specialize and center on changing the core of world philosophy. Individuals born at that time will fight for or against those changes in years ahead.

Chiron at 29 Scorpio: The adjustment here is that give and take has two sides. One who doesn't give should and one who doesn't take needs to learn to graciously accept.

North Node at 29 Scorpio: Must learn to give and to receive. Searching for balance between the material and spiritual.

South Node at 29 Scorpio: Must learn the value of love knowing that sex is not the total of love.

Sagittarius/Ninth House

Sagittarius is the sign of generosity and honesty. Any planet in Sagittarius will relate to both, positively or negatively. The twenty-ninth degree is in the Leo decan, taking on an air of pride combined with confidence. Sagittarius and Leo point to vastness but the strength is running out at the twenty-ninth degree (the game is about over) and may be restrictive. This is the dwad of Scorpio and only the native may be aware of any failures associated with the planet implied.

Sun at 29 Sagittarius: This is just before Christmas when one little light must shine very brightly to be noticed. The Sun at this degree has the capability to shine brightly. Optimism will carry the native through.

Moon at 29 Sagittarius: Emotionally extravagant or prone to depression. Has many female acquaintances at a distance. Seeks a companion who nurtures. May remain unattached in relationships. Likes spacious home.

Venus at 29 Sagittarius: Seeks extensively for whatever is pleasurable. Overextends socially. Is searching for an abundance of love without commitment.

Mercury at 29 Sagittarius: Communication is complicated. Native has difficulty in comprehension. Is childlike. Excellent wit. Likes travel. May succeed as writer.

Mars at 29 Sagittarius: Very much or very little outdoor activity. Is a spectator if not an athlete.

Jupiter at 29 Sagittarius: May become professional student or has difficulty in attaining certification and degrees. Travel is emphasized. Usually does not do well with in-laws. Enjoys legal teasing; flirts with breaking laws.

Saturn at 29 Sagittarius: Too little luck too much experience. Harnesses practicality with optimism and can be extremely successful. Is learning to be serious about life.

Uranus at 29 Sagittarius: Makes spontaneous changes in an effort to escape from any unpleasant situation. Creates own philosophy. Has a unique sense of humor.

Neptune at 29 Sagittarius: Loaded with excuses. Has back log of ideals not reached. Fantastic imagination, great for writing. Could have a problem deciphering truth from fiction.

Pluto 29 Sagittarius: Leader in the vast changes in religion. Pluto in Scorpio changes morals. Pluto in Sagittarius builds freedom of thoughts, seeking truth of spirit. Pluto was in early Scorpio in 1492 when Europeans began to come to North America for expression of morality, soon followed by the search for freedom of thought and religion through the transit of Pluto in Sagittarius.

Chiron at 29 Sagittarius: Escape is one of the keywords for Chiron. Sagittarius is tempted to run away. It is time to stay still and turn to psychology and faith.

North Node at 29 Sagittarius: Must hold to honesty, Learn to make use of knowledge and turn it into wisdom. To self be true.

South Node at 29 Sagittarius: Needs to avoid lawsuits. Needs to go back to the basics and use simple information.

Capricorn/Tenth house

Capricorn is the sign of experience and practical organization. Capricorn brings what is deserved, if the laws of honor have been followed honor will come. The Virgo decan influences the twenty-ninth degree, requiring precise organization. A 29 Capricorn planet may find the individual too cautious for too long and missing out on opportunity. This is the Sagittarius dwad which may allow forgetfulness to creep in.

Sun at 29 Capricorn: Too much or to6 little experience is imposed. May expect too much of self or may not be allowed the privilege to try. May have great burdens forced upon the native at an early age.

Moon at 29 Capricorn: Relates to service. Needs stable organization. Responsibility or sadness because of a woman or the family, yet attracted to women and home.

Venus at 29 Capricorn: Can't get enough business, regardless of how much or how little there is, still seeks more. People hold out on favors. Loves organizational work. Work is a favorite pastime.

Mercury at 29 Capricorn: Insatiable desire for information. Masses of paperwork surround this one. Record keeping is serious business. May be separated from a brother or sister, or has the responsibility of one.

Mars at 29 Capricorn: Salvages useable material or saves nothing. Probably works at more than one job. Too much or too little opportunity.

Jupiter at 29 Capricorn: Too much or too little education. Has much responsibility and has to learn the hard way how to handle it May make psychology the major business and be successful at it.

Saturn at 29 Capricorn: Can't get enough hard work. Enjoys working but runs into obstacles, or challenges. Is learning to be honorable because native is often exposed whether for criticism or for accomplishment.

Uranus at 29 Capricorn: Life's lessons will change frequently. Will be creative but will meet with many challenges in the making and distribution of products.

Neptune at 29 Capricorn: At the time of the current transit there will be much to do about drug and medical business. Those born at that time will wage battles concerning these issues pro and con. Generational politics will relate to church/state affairs, churches competing with citizens in tax exempt business.

Pluto at 29 Capricorn: Those having this degree in the natal chart will be extremely restless, or possibly powerful, concerning world transformation of corporate business.

Chiron at 29 Capricorn: The hard driving taskmaster has rebellious underlings. Honor comes to those who adjust to integrity rather than dictatorship.

North Node at 29 Capricorn: Must learn balance between career and family and learn to accept responsibility for success.

South Node at 29 Capricorn: Must learn purpose of responsibility and become aware of emotional sensitivity.

Aquarius/Eleventh House

Aquarius is the sign of individuality and freedom, and the twenty-ninth degree is in the Libra decan. The Aquarius free-spirit cannot feel free while trying to keep peace, which results in social frustrations. This is the Capricorn dwad, prompting the native to develop friendships which will produce fruitfully.

Sun at 29 Aquarius: Too much or too little social life. Could be restricted by someone else. Intuition is highly developed but not always trusted. Native needs encouragement.

Moon at 29 Aquarius: Too much or too little emotional freedom of expression. Seeks nurturing from friends. Swings between being friend and child of borrowed mother.

Venus at 29 Aquarius: Too much or too little enjoyment through friendships. Only wants a buddy not a sweetheart. Feels possessed in close attachments. Unique pleasures.

Mercury at 29 Aquarius: Wants new ideas but food for thought is limited. Gatherer of interesting and unusual information. Unusual sense of humor.

Mars at 29 Aquarius: Has need of companionship which would come through groups and clubs but is not comfortable there.

Jupiter at 29 Aquarius: Double freedom needed. Freedom for self and justice for all! Wants to be different but conforms through non-conforming activities in groups.

Saturn at 29 Aquarius: Learns through experiences of friend. Feels the responsibility of older persons. Is drawn to both the antiquated and the modern. Needs to learn to activate new ideas.

Uranus at 29 Aquarius: "Friends, Romans and countrymen, there is no discrimination in my friendships, but I may not take time for you."

Neptune at 29 Aquarius: Those born with this degree will be active in the process of world peace, by agreement or opposition. May be caught in the battle and become a victim.

Pluto at 29 Aquarius: Becomes attracted to powerful and important people or is intimidated by them. Could be good leader due to exposure to many, but does not want to be tied down by others.

Chiron at 29 Aquarius: Chiron, the Centaur, was also unique and he knew when it was time to make changes; sometimes the answer is "not yet."

North Node at 29 Aquarius: Needs to learn about love and romance and to recognize own creative talents. Can be self-centered.

South Node at 29 Aquarius: Love thy neighbor, but not romantically. Needs to learn deeper devotion in relationships and practice loyalty.

Pisces/Twelfth House

Pisces is the sign of devotion, also self undoing. The twenty-ninth degree is in the Scorpio decan. Both Pisces and Scorpio are willing to die for a good cause, consequently, devotion can become over-powering if under the influence of the twenty-nine degree planet. The dwad is Aquarius, sign of universal love. The strong devotion may well be for a universal cause such as a philosophy for improvement of life.

Sun at 29 Pisces: "All of me, why not take all of me?" Willing to sacrifice self for others. Has a feeling that every opportunity may be the last.

Moon at 29 Pisces: Skinny dipping is so soothing. A blessed nurturer, often without gratitude from the recipient. Usually loved by women but is not aware that it may be a deep love. Very psychic.

Venus at 29 Pisces: Say it with music. A poet at heart. Can love the unlovely. Money slips through the fingers.

Mercury at 29 Pisces: Exists on poetic reason. Interprets life through rose-colored glasses. Often blind to the truth and fully enjoys a secret which can be costly when harboring someone outside the law.

Mars at 29 Pisces: Can't get enough sympathy. Fools rush in where angels fear to tread. Gives beyond means. Buys much for self.

Jupiter at 29 Pisces: Not enough ideal justice. Always sees a thread of innocence in the worst of offenders. May be overly generous or gives only when returns are expected. The traveler.

Saturn at 29 Pieces: Too much or too little sympathy. Appears so competent no one suspects help is needed. Over schedules energy. Sadness through family.

Uranus at 29 Pisces: Miracles are everywhere but may not be recognized as such. Believes strongly in mind over matter and sees the mysteries of life manifested.

Neptune at 29 Pisces: "I'm a messiah!" or, "I believe in everything!" Neptune and Pisces—psychic communication. Planets in the twelfth house are telepathic. Persons who are born with Neptune at 29 should be able to send messages and receive even without a telephone.

Pluto at 29 Pisces: Pluto exposes and Pisces can be deceptive. People born with Pluto at 29° Pisces should be honest to the core and pledge energy toward purifying the world.

Chiron at 29 Pisces: Pisces is psychic and the adjustment may be to know who can be trusted and when not to be a martyr.

North Node at 29 Pisces: Needs to love self. Would benefit by accepting services from others.

South Node at 29 Pisces: Needs to avoid depressive people. The telepathic vibrations pick up depression and pain from others.

Chapter VIII

Cycles

Knowledge of the planetary cycles is helpful and by using these in relation to the natal chart, new insights can be gained. Following is the approximate length of time it takes for a planet to return to its natal placement:

1 year	Mercury
1 year	Venus
2 years	Mars
12 years	Jupiter
28 years	Saturn
84 years	Uranus
150 years	Neptune
240 years	Pluto

When the planet returns to the degree and minute of birth, a chart can be drawn to study the energy influence of the planet to cover the time up to the next cycle. The best text for this study is your own experience. You probably know about a solar (Sun) return and a lunar (Moon) return. You can make a Mercury return, Venus return, Mars return, Jupiter return, Saturn return and Uranus return (if you make it past age eighty-four) and study the cycles. You won't make it to celebrate your Neptune return or your Pluto return simply because of the time, but it is interesting to note the returns for those who have proceeded us.

It is suspected that the cycles have significance in the karmic interpretation, especially of planets which have karmic energy. If that planet is in southern declination or is retrograde, it is significant. As planets progress to new positions, karmic debts are cleared or put on hold for another lifetime, or we find ourselves in line to begin working on a new karmic debt in this lifetime. This can be seen in different ways. Suppose a planet is retrograde at birth. We have the opportunity to work on that karma immediately. If the planet progresses direct in motion we will either finish or resign the situation. If the planet is direct and progresses to retrograde, then we may begin working out a karmic condition. The same applies to planets in the declinations. If all planets are in declination at birth and there are no retrogrades, there would be very little early life karma until progressions activate something. If most of planets are in southern declination at birth and several planets are retrograde, there is much karma in the early life and it will lessen with age.

The planetary cycles listed above represent the planets by longitude. Declination cycles are the same in time with one-half of the journey would be in southern declination and the other half in northern declination. The Sun makes a complete cycle in one year and the Moon makes a complete cycle in about twenty-eight days. From the spring equinox to the autumnal equinox the Sun is in northern declination then from autumn back to spring the Sun is in southern declination.

The Moon makes a complete cycle in about twenty-eight days. Fourteen days in northern declination and fourteen days in southern declination.

The Nodes complete a cycle in eighteen and a half years. Generally only the North Node is listed in the ephemeris, but the South Node is exactly opposite it; same degree, same minute, opposite sign.

Chapter IX

A Karmic Study

A review of the life of a remarkable individual, Edgar Cayce, reveals an overview of karma as he lived it. Following this review you will be shown an application of each of the seven areas discussed to the interpretation of any individual's karma.

Communicating with the Dead

It is reported that at about age six or seven, he announced he was communicating with relatives and friends who had died and was able to see them. A solar return for 1883, age six, shows transiting Saturn conjunct Pluto. Natal Saturn (lessons to be learned) is in Pisces in southern declination. Now the teacher, Saturn, comes to the money sign, Taurus, conjunct natal Pluto in the tenth house. This conjunction has a karmic message concerning money. His fame as a healer also brought him money. Pluto in the tenth house is an indication the native will do something among the masses which will change things and people. It also implies that the individual will be known after death for something. As we look at the natal chart, we see that Saturn was conjunct natal Neptune perhaps two years earlier and then conjunct the Moon. These were in the natal ninth house of visions and imagery. It is strongly suspected that the child had been experiencing these spirit playmates and friends for much longer than he had let be known.

That same 1883 solar return shows transiting South Node conjunct natal Moon. South Node is representative of past life contacts and experiences. This is a time when Edgar would have become sensitive to women and their ailments. Note here that Neptune has just passed a conjunction to the natal Moon calling upon him to be sympathetic toward women.

Learning by Osmosis

At age nine, the youngster discovered that he could place a book under his head and sleep the knowledge into his memory bank. The solar return for 1886 has transiting Neptune exactly conjunct natal Pluto in the eighth house of mysteries. The Moon and Mars are in the twelfth house between the natal South Node and the transiting North Node, while the transiting South Node is exactly conjunct natal Venus in Pisces in the fifth house. Venus is the ruler of his third house of his natal chart, the mind. Chiron in Gemini in the solar return chart is square the Moon and Mars in the eleventh which says, "Alter knowledge in reference to others." Meanwhile, Mars of the solar return is retrograding over natal South Node. Again we see the South Node launching past experience toward destiny. The ninth year of life is when the Nodes are at a half cycle, that is, the North Node is

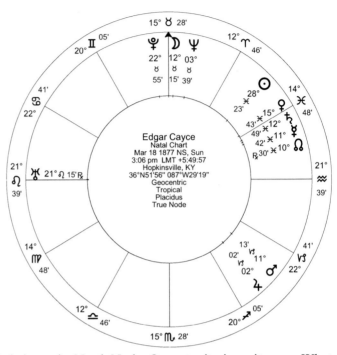

on the South Node and the South Node is on the North Node. Opportunity is on its way. What will he do with it?

How does this event fit into the remainder of his life? It seems that after he was out of school, he no longer had the ability. Did he no longer have it or did he no longer use it? At any rate, he had proof through experience that the mind could perform uniquely. This was a forerunner for the confidence he was to have in his talent.

Lost His Voice (April 18, 1900)

The next incident we review is so impressive it is difficult to know where and how to begin. Sometime during the day of April 18, 1900 Edgar Cayce, while employed as a salesperson, lost his voice. His general health held up and he changed jobs. He could not speak for almost ten months. There are three charts that explain this event: solar return for 1900, natal progressed to April 18, 1900 and diurnal for April 18, 1900, each of which follow:

Let's begin with the progressed chart. Saturn, being lessons in life, has progressed to conjunct natal Venus (vocal chords) on the eighth house cusp of the natal chart and in the eleventh house of the karmic horoscope. The eighth house represents major change and the eleventh is goals and aspirations, in Pisces they were probably unknown at the time. Sun was progressed to 21 Aries 05 within one degree of the karmic Ascendant at 20 Aries 19 and within minutes trine both natal ascendant and natal Uranus. Just three months previously the progressed Moon had passed over the progressed Venus/Saturn conjunction and at the end of the ten months, when the

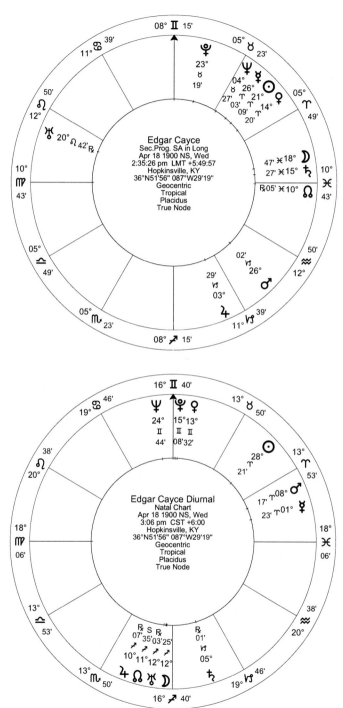

voice was recovered, the progressed Moon was exactly conjunct natal Sun at 28 Pisces 23—new beginnings. Progressed Ascendant was within one degree of the natal South Node (karma). Progressed Neptune was on the progressed ninth house cusp; Neptune (sleep) and ninth house (mental travels).

Now look at the diurnal for April 18, 1900. A diurnal chart keeps all of the birth data except the date of interest, in this case the date he lost his voice. Pluto is within one degree of the Midheaven in Gemini (communications). Venus is in the ninth house conjunct the South Node (karma). Directly opposite is the North Node then Moon by minutes conjunct Uranus, then Jupiter only two degrees away. That is five planets and the Nodes within a five degree orb. Drop Jupiter and it is only three degrees. All of this receives an exact "T" from natal Mercury, Saturn and Venus. Something had to happen!

Neptune, Uranus, Saturn and Pluto, the outer planets are prominent in his karmic activities. Pluto and Uranus and Saturn are in this cluster. Jupiter has progressed to seven minutes trine to natal Neptune saying "everything is going to be all right." In the diurnal, Neptune sits alone in the tenth house clapping his hands (Gemini) knowing that a new guru is being initiated.

Now we look at the solar return for 1900 and find natal seventh house rising with natal Uranus falling in the sixth house very near the seventh cusp. Sun is intercepted in the first house with transiting Mars (attack) conjunct Venus (voice), Mercury (communication) and Saturn (work lesson) of the natal chart. Sun and Mars intercepted announce that he would be closed into himself during the year. The duplicated house cusps are Cancer and Capricorn, on the fifth (creativity) and sixth (health) and eleventh (the unusual) and twelfth (privacy) houses. Saturn, ruler of Capricorn, is in its own sign conjunct natal Jupiter. This is one of the most fortunate transits to organize life. The Moon in Scorpio is in the eighth

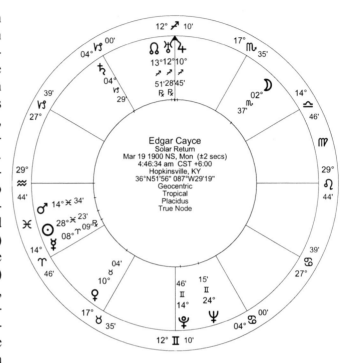

house of the solar return and opposite mute natal Neptune. Because of the focus on an opposition, regardless of how dark and private the situation is, Scorpio and Neptune, in this case, is always become aware in due time. An opposition is like a full Moon giving light at night when it is needed. It is time to stop playing around with Mars in the natal chart, and get down to the business of life.

Going back to Venus (the voice), it is natally at 15 Pisces 43. In the solar return, the Nodes are at 15 Sagittarius/Gemini 03. Any time a planet is in the same degree as the Nodes, that planet requires attention. The Nodes T-square natal Venus conjunct solar return Mars and solar return Pluto is conjunct the South Node—karma. Solar return Uranus is within three degrees of the North Node. This is important later.

The time of day that he lost his voice is not known but knowing the date we look back at the diurnal chart again. Natal Venus, which was at 15 Pisces 43, forms a square with the 1900 solar return Nodes at 15 Sagittarius/Gemini 03. It is particularly significant when the South Node is in the same degree as a natal planet because of the karmic energy activated; also, his progressed Saturn, 15 Pisces 27, was conjunct his natal Venus at 15 Pisces 43 and is also conjunct his solar return Mars at 14 Pisces 34. Pluto in the solar return is at 14 Gemini 46 conjunct the South Node at 15 Gemini 03.

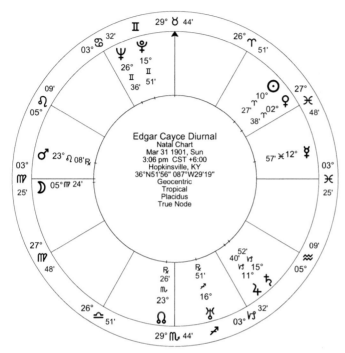

Recovered His Voice

According to the two dates given in reference to this event, his voice was inactive for eleven months and thirteen days, from March 18, 1900 to March 31, 1901. There was a series of events that culminated in a hypnotist of some experience conducting as suggested by a physician which resulted in the origin of what Cayce called a reading. To quote from that reading, ". . . due to a partial paralysis of the inferior muscles of the vocal cords, produced by nerve strain. This is a psychological condition producing a physical effect. This may be removed by increasing circulation . . ." The secret was self-hypnosis with someone to give information and data and no commands. Note: The author both as a hypnotist and an astrologer can plainly see how it would be near impossible to hypnotize anyone with Uranus conjunct a Leo Ascendant, which is not inclined to take orders from anyone.

The remarkable mutable "T" square that was activated when his voice was lost had changed by recovery time. Jupiter had advanced to conjunct natal Mars (muscle). Uranus one week earlier made a retrograde station and at recovery was one degree opposition to Pluto. Saturn (lesson), not in the "T" was at 5 Capricorn in the voice lost diurnal moved to 15 Capricorn and square Progressed Venus (voice) in Aries. Mercury (nerve) in the voice lost diurnal is one degree conjunct Venus in the voice return diurnal. Also, the Nodes were hovering the fourth/tenth cusps. He set forth almost immediately looking for some business and chose photography, ruled Neptune. Neptune was sitting three minutes from the Ascendant of his 1901 solar return, two degrees from a square to return Sun in the tenth house. It looks like he picked correctly.

Impressive factors occurred in the progressed chart to uphold business change. Saturn had progressed to conjunct his natal Venus in the eighth house, saying "time to go into business." The Moon had progressed into 0 Aries. Zero degree of any cardinal sign is always activated, even if it stands alone and is just waiting for a lunar transit.

Although Edgar Cayce never wrote a book, he was persuaded to write something about how he got into his work and it amounted to about twenty pages. He made it clear in that writing that the loss of his voice and his own diagnosis and treatment for his recovery was the origin of his career as a psychic reader.

Jupiter Return

Jupiter at 03 Capricorn 12 made its second return on January 28, 1901 at 8:37 p.m. A Jupiter return is effective for twelve years, until the next return. Looking at the Jupiter return chart, it should be no surprise to see Pluto within three degrees of the Midheaven, minutes from an opposition with Uranus three degrees from the fourth house cusp. The return Jupiter in the business sign (Capricorn) is in the fourth house which it rules. This indicates that the next job may be in the home. The Moon at 0 Gemini in the ninth house is another indicator of a move to a distant place (Bowling Green was a distant move at that time).

Referencing the March 31, 1901 diurnal chart, cast for when his voice returned, we see another note concerning the Nodes as they hovered the fourth/tenth house cusps, which can bring a karmic change to the public image. The Nodes of the Jupiter return chart were in the same degree of his natal Sun. There is a philosophical theory in some circles that before one can soar to the highest levels, the bottom must be touched. Cayce had bottomed out! There was no way to go but up!

Moved to Bowling Green

In 1902, Cayce took a job in a book store in Bowling Green, Kentucky. We have found these planets to be consistently involved when his karmic pathway is activated—-Neptune, Uranus and Pluto, and of course, the Moon. These are the planets nearest the angles in his natal chart. In the solar return for 1902 Uranus is in the 4th house indicating the move, Pluto in the tenth house shows change and the new job is represented by Mercury at 0 Pisces in the sixth house. Mars at 0 Aries in the seventh house which could give us to suspect that he would soon be courting.

Neptune was in the tenth house at 28 Gemini, within minutes of a square to the Sun in the seventh house and, of course, in the sign that Neptune rules. This no doubt awakened him to a potential mate. The Moon, which indicates women, opposes Jupiter at 8 Aquarius; they both square the Nodes at 6 Scorpio and Taurus. Since the Moon rules the eleventh house, and is in the degree of the nodes, it is safe to assume that the event would involve a woman friend.

Leo rules pleasure and entertainment and that year, Cayce sold a parlor game to Parker Brothers for a respectable fee. Since so few of us have known anyone who has developed and sold a game, let's look at it. Games are Gemini or Leo, third or fifth house. In Cayce's 1902 solar return, Jupiter rules his fourth house (home) and is in the fifth house of fun. Jupiter is trine Pluto in Gemini in the tenth house, and Pluto rules the third house of board games.

Marriage

On June 17, 1903, Edgar Cayce married Gertrude Evans. Pluto is in the seventh house in the degree of the Nodes in the 1903 solar return chart. The South Node at 17 Aries is conjunct his progressed Venus at 18 Aries. He encounters a karmic relationship. Lessons to be learned or a job to be done are shown by Saturn. Venus is in the eighth house of his natal chart and within a three degree orb of being conjunct Saturn which is in the seventh house. Venus in the 1903 solar return, representing money, is at 24 Aries in the fifth house, within one degree of a perfect trine

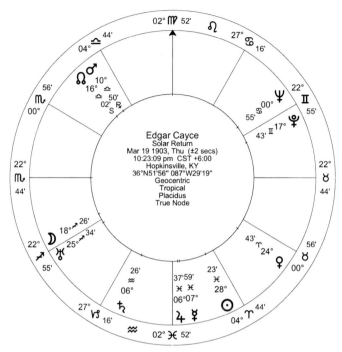

to Uranus in the second house, bringing unexpected income. As we continue to follow the karma we will see that it was her perseverance that brought money into the union. Venus rules his 3rd house and his tenth house. This configuration would add up to a friend/wife who is serious by nature, perhaps a bit older, and certainly takes part in his business. Since Saturn is in the natal seventh he would be destined to be subject to someone who would control and be responsible for him, not to mention tying him down, something not a hundred percent appreciated by Uranus on the natal Ascendant.

Points to note in the diurnal chart are house cusps. Venus is only half a degree from the tenth house cusp and in the sign of romantic Leo, accompanied by an interesting eighth house for a wedding day. Mercury, Pluto and the Sun in Gemini (talk, talk, talk) and Neptune in Cancer? Neptune rules the fifth house. Can we get children by just talking? Seriously, Venus has just entered the tenth house; business is changing.

He had not been in Bowling Green very long and here he is making more changes in the home. Aquarius is on the fourth house cusp and Saturn had moved into the third by eighteen minutes. Note that Saturn moved into the third house because the wheel moves one direction and the planets the other. Looking at a diurnal chart for the previous day, June 16, Saturn would still be in the fourth house. Communications in the home are described by Saturn in Aquarius in the third house of the diurnal chart on the wedding day. These communications will bring in money in a short time because Uranus rules the fourth house but is in the second house of money.

After the Moon moves three degrees it will square Uranus. The Moon was square Pluto and energizing Pluto in the eighth house just one degree earlier. Pluto rules the diurnal Ascendant, Scorpio. Venus is the elevated planet allowing the wife to be in charge. How do we know Venus is the wife? Because it is his diurnal not hers, nor is it the wedding chart per se. Venus rules the seventh house.

Neptune is in Cancer in the eighth house. Psychic energies, including privacy and research, will no doubt be moving into the home. The Nodes are in the sixth and twelfth houses but will very shortly be in the fifth and eleventh, insuring that the partnership will be built on friendship and creativity, which makes for a far more solid relationship than lust. The marriage diurnal set the scene for the next important event involving Cayce's karma.

At some time along the way Edgar Cayce's friend Dr. Al Layne in Hopkinsville apparently asked help with a patient. The Bowling Green newspaper carried an impressive write-up on June 22, 1903, just five days after the marriage. The write-up referred to Cayce's ability to go to sleep at which time he would diagnose physical conditions, and further, that he had rendered that service to Dr. Layne. From then until his death the story was the same: Cayce in trance . . . patient healed . . . public amazed.

Need for Freedom or Individuality

In 1912, Edgar Cayce tried to stop doing psychic medical readings but it did not work. The solar return chart had one obvious content. Mercury at the thirteenth degree of a cardinal sign in the third house. A crisis must be met and decided. He evidently wanted and needed more time for himself, Mercury was in Aries. Now all he had to do was conjure up a way to get that time. It would not be easy. The Nodes in Aries and Libra insist on time with others and the South Node in Libra holds sway toward others but the best path is toward self. because of the North Node's location in Aries. There was a Jupiter return on January 11, 1913. Cayce now wanted to stop what he had started with the last Jupiter return on January 28, 1901.

In 1914, there was a solar eclipse at 15 Pisces 29 that was the second nodal return since birth; Cayce was age thirty-eight. In that return Chiron was at 15 Pisces 29 (do you remember that degree in 1900 when fate took over his voice?) conjunct the North Node in the eighth house. The message was that it was time to work on issues related to survival. Looking at the 1914 solar return, we see that the Sun was in the eighth house in Pisces (compassion), the Ascendant was in Leo, as at birth, the Moon was twenty-one minutes from natal Mars in the fifth house, where Mars was at birth, and now return Mars in the eleventh house is only minutes from a perfect opposition to Cayce's natal mars. As occurred in the past, a friend was responsible for putting him back into trances. This is without a doubt a part of his karma.

Reincarnation

Life readings opening new information to the western world on the subject of reincarnation, were discovered in the fall of 1923 when Uranus transited Cayce's Pisces stellium. During that year Jupiter would transit the natal chart going through a series of trine aspects to each of the five planets in the Pisces stellium. Pluto spends thirty years transiting the sign of Cancer and would spend the next fifteen years in transit trine the natal North Node at 09 Pisces 53, then trine natal Mercury at 11 Pisces 42, then trine natal Saturn at 12 Pisces 49, then trine natal Venus at 15 Pisces 43 and make the last trine with the natal Sun at 28 Pisces 23 in 1938; then Pluto finally moves on along.

When transiting Neptune made a retrograde station on his natal ascendant 1925, Cayce moved his facilities to Virginia Beach, Virginia. Neptune rules his Sun sign (Pisces) and therefore it is his life's ruler.

He had well established and administered his karmic assignments by the time of his death on January 3, 1945. The work and readings of Edgar Cayce introduced the Western Hemisphere to karma and reincarnation in an acceptable manner. He made his transition from this life on January 3, 1945, near our precession into the New Age, the Age of Aquarius. This is significant when we note that Uranus on his Ascendant.

In this section we have seen Cayce's karma unfold. In Section III, we will study Cayce's horoscope and apply these key areas to the karma of his life thus learn to do our own karmic reading.

The Karmic Degree

Edgar Cayce became famous through his many health readings. As a part of these, Cayce applied the precepts of karma and reincarnation for his clients. In this regard it seems fitting that we use his chart as we complete our study of the karmic horoscope and the evaluation of the karma degree.

The midpoint between the Sun and the Moon in Cayce's chart that places the Sun above the horizon is the karmic degree for a male. This point in Cayce's chart is 20 Aries 19 for the Ascendant. Isidore Kozminsky in *Zodiacal Symbology and Its Planetary Power* defines that degree as, "Under the influence of the planet Mars. A man struggling with a fierce serpent whilst others armed with large knives are hurrying to aid him. Denotes one who will be assailed by secret and open enemies, who will be liable to troubles and false accusation. In his dealings he should always exercise great care, and should not rely on word-of-mouth agreements. He will not be without devoted friends, who will not neglect him in the hour of his greatest need. His intense feelings will cause him trouble, danger, illness, and regret, and he will have to strive with the dark serpent. Let him unite himself with noble and good-living people, and put away from himself votaries [devotee or worshiper] of evil. It is a symbol of Contention."

Certainly Cayce met with opposition much of his life. Especially unkind were people of the medical profession. Medical students at one point invited him to come to their study group for experiments and while he was in trance they put him a refrigerated unit and almost killed him with over exposure. He was arrested, persecuted, and ignored in the cruelest ways, and yet, he pushed forward in his mission of life.

The Ascendant degree, 20 Aries 19, is in the Sagittarius decan and the Sagittarius dwad. He was a Sunday school teacher and carried a bible most of his life. His faith was strong and his philosophy expansive. He was a traveler, and his air of confidence brought him success in business ventures, although there were struggles. With Sagittarius, things are large, and when Cayce had a problem, it was usually enormous.

The karmic chart holds Neptune in the first house pointing to his interest in photography which from time to time was his main source or income. It of course depicts his ability as a psychic. The Moon which is also in the first house, enhances this psychic ability, especially since it is in trine with Mars in the ninth house (of prophecy). The karmic chart fits with the natal chart which has Jupiter in its natural ninth house trine Neptune coming back into the first house.

Uranus is in the fifth house in Leo, allowing a unique expression of ego and self-esteem. The eleventh house stellium upholds the fact that his friends were also business (Saturn) clients who consulted (Mercury) him for pay (Venus). A greater concentration of planets lies in the eleventh house in Pisces: Mercury, Saturn and Venus tightly conjunct. He is to be mentally aware of the needs of friends. He is to learn from these experiences. He is to cherish and honor his own aspirations.

The Sun is in the twelfth house in Pisces. This is appropriate for a man known as "The Sleeping Prophet." The Moon in Taurus in the first house says that he will karmically deal with emotional control concerning self and earning ability.

Jupiter and Mars in the ninth in the business sign of Capricorn provided Cayce with business from distant places; many readings came to him as a result of widespread newspaper publicity. Since he was a threat to the medical profession, it was often necessary for him to suddenly pack up and run for his own safety.

The Aries Ascendant introduces him as a pioneer of something. Pluto, which indicates the pioneering change, is in the second house and rules the eighth (psychic research), which signifies the income of his works even after his death.

There are two signatures in the fifth house of children. One of his sons inherited his keen interest in issues of the unique nature as implied by Uranus in the fifth, while the other expressed more interest in the business control factors and research of Atlantis, as indicated by the South Node in Virgo. Both of Cayce's sons, Hugh Lynn and Edgar Evans, have written about their famous father. Thanks to them the research library in Virginia Beach, the Association for Research and Enlightenment (A.R.E.), continues to function.

So, the karmic degree chart is interpreted much as you would a natal chart. It conflicts with none of the natal chart, provided the birth time is accurate. It adds more insight, more detail and more understanding. It has been found that when there are significant events, changes or attitudes in life that there is a planet pertaining to that energy progressed or transiting in aspect to the karmic degree in most circumstances. Some examples will be given in the interpretation of Edgar Cayce's chart later.

The equal house karmic degree chart can be turned to interpret any phase of life. As an example, to analyze work or health, turn the karmic degree chart so that the karmic degree is on the sixth house cusp. On Cayce's karmic degree chart, this would cause Scorpio to fall on the Ascendant. Jupiter and Mars would be in the second house showing that money went out as fast as it came in. The Pisces stellium in the fourth house (North Node, Mercury, Saturn and Venus) allowed him to do readings at home. The Sun in the fifth house gave him pride in his children, but Pisces accounted for his being ashamed of his ability for a long time. Aries is on the sixth house cusp;

Neptune and the Moon in the sixth house perfectly describe his work. Neptune tells of his psychic work and the Moon indicates the thousands of people who sought his assistance. Pluto in the seventh house establishes the strength of his partner and the power of persuasion of others over him. Uranus in the tenth house tells us he had unusual ability and pride in his work. In time, Uranus turned retrograde and Cayce became less public.

Karmic Lessons of Saturn

Saturn represents the lesson we came into this life to learn or our major mission in life. Since Saturn rules time and the past, we must associate experiences from the past with the lesson. I have found very little information on any past lifetimes of Edgar Cayce but Saturn in Pisces and the Nodes in Virgo and Pisces would indicate that he would have been involved with institutional business, very likely an equivalent to hospitals in his most recent lifetime. With Saturn conjunct Mercury and Venus now he would be learning to communicate in these areas and would develop a loving compassion for the people with whom he worked. He would also be challenged by contacts with authority figures connected with institutions. His lesson is in compassionate humility.

Anyone who has read anything about Mr. Cayce knows that he worked himself to exhaustion for those who could benefit from his services and he made extensive effort toward preserving general information which would be valuable to any others who may have a similar condition.

We can make various assumptions about past life experiences by way of Saturn. Had the former soul abused patients and now has chosen to compensate for his soul's error? Did he have an opportunity to do the things he did in the current lifetime in a previous life and refused to become involved? Was he confined in an institution or a prison and the soul remembers the episode with a promise to assist others in an escape by his services? Or was he simply magnifying and adding to his ability as a psychic with much healing ability much like a master called Jesus? Do we know? What we do know is that he set up a total lifetime in which he could learn compassionate humility. Obviously he chalked up some soul growth in the lifetime with which we are familiar (1877 to 1945).

Quoting from *Zodiacal Symbology* by Isidore Kozminsky, the symbology for Saturn's degree (12 Pisces 49) is, "A man crossing a bog on an old tree which has long ago fallen. Denotes one who meets with public favor and support whose temper will be severely tried and tested. Although possessed of radical feelings, he will find himself compelled by circumstances to obtain conservative support even though that support be grudgingly given. Still it will serve. It is a symbol of Preserving." This quote is appropriate to Cayce's Saturn. From this quote we could suspect that he began schooling through Saturn in these subjects in former lifetimes and graduated to a much higher level in the most recent life.

Cayce's Karma Through Retrogrades

Uranus is the only planet retrograde in the natal chart. Retrogrades represent vibrations which were incomplete in the past. This lifetime provides an opportunity for completion. A retrograde may imply something poorly done which is to be repeated and perfected in the present.

Uranus is unique different or original in nature. Since there is nothing new under the Sun, we could say it is a renewal of something that appears to be new. Uranus falls in the fifth house of creativity in the karmic degree chart. This offers energy for creativity through something original, unusual or new. The ego will be at stake because Uranus is in Leo in the fifth house. This will be done because Uranus sits within minutes of the Ascendant in the natal chart,

Natally Uranus is conjunct the Ascendant and in the twelfth house. We then can double the emphasis of the degree symbology. Again, quoting from *Zodiacal Symbology* for 21 Leo 15 (natal Uranus) is, "A man carrying a bird in a golden cage. Denotes one who is in danger of being held in restraint of some kind and of being moved to different places at the will of others. There is no suggestion of unkind treatment, but there is that the native is not a free agent. He should never permit others to gain influence over him in any way. He is very mediumistic, but can be controlled from the visible as he can from the invisible. It is a symbol of Restriction."

Though there was only one planet retrograde at birth, Mercury and Jupiter progressed retrograde and Uranus progressed direct in his lifetime. Retrogrades bring us to grips with issues from the past or to the present development of things already launched. Uranus retrograde on the ascendant says, "You are born out of your time because there is nothing new on the earth and you keep presenting what appears to be too new for acceptance. You are different, learn to take advantage of it." Uranus progressed direct in 1917. He had experienced half a Saturn cycle since Dr. Layne led him into hypnosis which allowed him to cure himself of an eleven month mute situation. By 1917 he was full time into health readings, including many absent readings. He finally had to accept that he was unique and was stuck with it.

Jupiter progressed retrograde in 1909 about the time more professionally certified people began to ridicule him and by 1912 he tried to abandon his talent. But Jupiter was in southern declination . . . karmic! It was the year following the Sun progressing into Taurus. He never was told by the President of the Karmic Universe that he couldn't make money at it. It was October 9, 1910 that the *New York Times* printed two pages of headlines and pictures about the "wonder man." Jupiter rules newspapers.

Mercury, direct at birth, progressed retrograde in 1934. February 3, 1935, Edgar Cayce made a rare appearance and presented a talk in Washington, D.C. The title was "Soul Power." He boldly stated, "For I am determined that as long as I live I will know nothing among men save Jesus Christ and Him crucified!" How did this event identify with a retrograde Mercury? He reiterated his belief. A word beginning with "re" usually expresses Mercury retrograde. There are 14,246 transcribed tapes of Mr. Cayce's readings on record in the A.R.E. Library but you are advised not to join so many who in error make reference to books "by Edgar Cayce." Neither Edgar Cayce nor Jesus ever wrote a book. For more information on retrogrades, see the author's book *Understanding Retrogrades*.

Karma of the Twenty-ninth Degree

Edgar Cayce had neither a planet nor a house cusp in the twenty-ninth degree. It is well to remember that the Moon progresses to the twenty-ninth degree approximately every two years, four months, where we all get a small taste of twenty-ninth degree karma. We will look at the progressions of the Sun, Mercury, Venus and Mars to demonstrate karma as they were the only planets, other than the Moon, to progress to the twenty-ninth degree during Cayce's lifetime.

Mercury progressed to the twenty-ninth degree of psychic Pisces in 1906. Within a year, as Mercury progressed into Aries, Venus progressed to the same degree of Pisces. The twenty-ninth degree often conveys a finishing element. It was during these years that his childhood ability of extreme psychic experiences lessened considerably. The twenty-ninth degree of Pisces is in the eighth house of the natal chart which represents communication with spirits, and in the twelfth house of the karmic degree chart which is representative of telepathic psychic talents.

The collective publicity, which appeared in a 1910 newspaper article, had been collected and prepared the previous year when the Sun was at 29 Aries. The twenty-ninth degree of Aries fell in the ninth house of the natal chart interestingly representing newspapers. And the twenty-ninth degree of Aries fell in the first house of the Karmic Degree chart; the articles were about him personally.

Venus progressed to 29 Aries in 1912, when he wanted to quit doing health readings. The news article mentioned above brought more clients as the Sun progressed into Taurus and one event following another found him still at it many years later. This twenty-ninth degree is in the same houses as referenced in the paragraph above.

In 1936, Venus progressed to 29 Taurus in the tenth house of the natal chart and the second house of the karmic degree chart, affecting his finances. As a result, in 1937 Cayce began to make a few public appearances which closed his Taurus territorial privacy and opened up his communications as Venus moved into Gemini.

Mars was progressed to the twenty-ninth degree for two years, 1905 and 1906, at which time Cayce, his wife and their friend Dr. Al Layne where dedicated to training Cayce and recording his readings. The twenty-ninth degree of Capricorn is in his sixth house of both health and work in the natal chart, and appropriately, in the tenth house of the karmic degree chart; this is appropriate since his career had evolved to the area of health.

Cayce's Karma Through the Nodes

The purpose of the lifetime is shown by the Nodes. Edgar Cayce's Nodes are in Pisces and Virgo. This is the polarity of service, hearing, compassion and commitment. There is a need to find a balance in serving and being served. This polarity frequently seeks an outlet through interests related to health.

Cayce had the South Node in Virgo, which is routine, perfection, discrimination, sanitation, order and analyzation, all of which were familiar to his nature. The North Node in Pisces calls for going with, as opposed to, a routine; associating with the imperfect, that is with the ill, rather than demanding a perfect environment; accepting people for what they are, rather than discriminating against them; looking through the impurities for the cause versus concentrating on a lack of proper sanitation; and being willing to disrupt order to forward the cause thus allowing the psychic to emerge, rather than trying to analyze practicality.

In the natal chart the Nodes fall in the first and seventh houses with the South Node in the first. Cayce's need was to recognize the value of the partner and co-workers and to share himself with those around him. He was to keep himself above reproach in his close relationships (Virgo) and to associate with people of sympathy and understanding (Pisces).

The Nodes in the karmic degree horoscope fall in the fifth and eleventh houses with the Virgo South Node in the fifth bringing with it the knowledge of dealing with ego and the ability to be creative. If the native uses the energy brought into the present lifetime by the North Node in Pisces in the eleventh house of hopes and wishes, there is attainment of goals set. A proof of this is that a close friend put him back on track twice during his lifetime.

If an individual starts early in life to build on past experiences of the South Node in working toward fulfillment of the North Node, then added peace, ease and pleasure will result sooner in life. The potential result of the Virgo/Pisces or Pisces/Virgo nodal path can indeed be the miracle worker and provides for faith and spiritual healing.

Edgar Cayce's Declinations and His Karma

It would have been too confusing to have tried to mix declinations with the interpretations on the preceding pages. Planets in southern declination describe karma. Edgar Cayce had six planets in southern declination. They are: Sun, 0S39; Venus, 6S56; Saturn, 8S19; Mercury, 9S16; Jupiter, 23S01; and Mars, 23S25.

A special note: On the declination scale, any planet located between 0N00 and 14N22 is said to be in the talent section of a declination chart and any planet located 14N22 and outward in northern declination is said to be in the power section of a declination chart.

Edgar Cayce had Neptune, Pluto and Chiron in the talent section of the declination scale. Through Neptune he received psychic impressions, idealism, compassion, and psychic ability; Pluto .gave him the talent to close himself totally away from the world and to go not to the interior of the Earth but to the heights of Spirit; Chiron brought those who needed him to his doorstep, or him to theirs, as the case may have been. Anyone who pays any attention to Chiron would have to accept the validity of the healer and health advisor for this interpretation. We believe that Chiron also calls for an adjustment of some kind. At birth Chiron was at 27 Aries 58; he certainly had to make an adjustment in the personal life due to the strangeness of his ability.

The Moon and Uranus are found in the power section. Moon provided power of the public and his charisma. Uranus endowed him with perhaps the most unique power of the twentieth century.

The Sun is at 0S39, in Pisces by sign. The Pisces Sun expresses through other persons more than directly through self. Two years after birth the Sun progressed into northern declination and in the sign of Aries. Energy here allows personal direction of life and a bit of courage.

Venus is in southern declination at 6S56, also in the sign of Pisces, and usually brings with it the karma of relationships. These may be friends, lovers, business associates, or family members, including children. In other words, anybody you loved from the past. Venus progressed into the Northern declination just before age fifteen, but longitudinally had progressed into the sign of Aries the previous year. This crossover from southern declination would have allowed

Cayce to complete karma with someone or something. He went to work on a farm soon after his fifteenth birthday.

Mercury is in southern declination at 9S16 and in the sign of Pisces. Mercury in southern declination promotes karma concerning communications. It was about the time Mercury and Venus were going into Aries and crossing over into northern declination that Cayce discovered he could no longer glean information from books by putting them under his pillow and sleeping on them.

Mercury had progressed into northern declination at about age twelve, when it also progressed into Aries by longitude. In addition to the crossover from southern to northern declination and the longitudinal sign change, at age forty-six in 1923, Mercury progressed out-of-bounds and that was the year he discovered that he was being exposed to reincarnation and karma in his readings. How apropos, out-of-bounds gives ability beyond the expected!

How do these progressions effect karma? During those early years when he was experiencing psychic impressions and getting actions and reactions from people around him. Northern declination supplied karmic protection and energy for talent to develop.

For a moment let's look at some of Saturn's aspect by longitude. Saturn inconjunct Mercury and Venus (stability); Saturn is sextile the Moon, favoring good relationships with both men and women; and Saturn is applying to a sextile with Mars which is supportive of good business. Mars in Capricorn in the ninth house describes philosophers, educators and professional people, such as those of the medical field, all being available for involvement in his karmic mission. We could well add to this list the news media, many of whom wished to make him a laughing-stock which inadvertently favored Cayce, and caused the public to flock to him. Now let's get back to declinations. Saturn is parallel Mercury in southern declination. By the time the publicity was occurring in 1910 Saturn by declination had progressed to a parallel to natal Venus at 6S56. Progressed Venus at 9N10 was contraparallel natal Mercury at 9S16. The difficulties that were brought by the contraparallel were magnified favorably by the parallel. Note that it is Saturn that is parallel and remember that it is Saturn that gives us what we deserve.

Jupiter is also in the karmic southern declination. Here we find that he held on to his philosophy as a diligent bible student as he traveled and taught. Jupiter served as ground work for the early years stimulating generosity in sharing healing information, Jupiter was at 23S01 at birth and had progressed only four minutes by his death. Any planet beyond twenty-three degrees declination, even if it does not go out-of-bounds, seems to promise a destiny of achievement relative to that planet. Some of his achievements relative to Jupiter were, his religion, his generosity, his travels, his advanced knowledge and his ability to "see" (as the motto for Sagittarius would represent).

Mars in southern declination in Capricorn allowed him to be serious about his life, but not without strife. At birth Mars was at 23S25 within two minutes of being out-of-bounds and was going toward the lower degrees. However, on the day preceding birth Mars was out-of-bounds and remained so (by converse direction) until he was age twenty-four. The year would have been 1901, the year that he regained his voice, as related in the previous Section of this book. When we were told by a student that Cayce had a breakdown my immediate response was, "I don't see it." Neither Mercury nor Uranus are sufficiently activated to indicate such; it must have been at a different time. When Mars progressed back in bounds (conversely) something had to be strongly significant. A muscle was binding a nerve relative to the vocal cords. Relaxation and a command for blood to flow to the affected area allowed for immediate healing.

From our list of favorite asteroids, we chose Kassandra, Sphinx, Sisyphus, Atlantis and Pandora to analyze a crises in the life of Edgar Cayce.

The god Apollo endowed Kassandra with the gift of prophecy but later cursed her by proclaiming that no one would believe what she said. We can imagine Mr. Cayce's psychological dilemma; he believed that his visions were true but realized that he would be ridiculed if he related them. His natal Kassandra was positioned at 0 Taurus 27 and 8N38, contraparallel both natal Saturn at 8S49 and natal Mercury at 9S16, which probably explains the halting pattern of his speech when in a trance. The 1901 progressed Sun was at 8N36 parallel natal Kassandra. His ego had to reckon with his gift of prophecy, but how? His 1901 solar return reveals Kassandra at 27 Sagittarius 34 within twenty-four minutes of an exact trine to natal Chiron, thus compelling him to use his talent for healing. Those persons who subsequently benefitted from his diagnostic readings didn't care whether the medical community or anybody else believed it; they knew they were in better health afterwards.

The asteroid Sphinx is astrologically identified with the phrase "unsolved mysteries." The Sphinx sits in the dessert and sees all but, being stone, tells nothing. Cayce's visions of the past and the future were uncomfortable but he could not stop them. His natal Sphinx at 3 Pisces 30 is in sextile aspect to natal Neptune at 3 Taurus 39, and its declination at 5S13 is contraparallel natal Pluto at 4N58. His psyche was tuned to unraveling the mysteries of the Earth (both planets in Taurus), but Sphinx preferred to remain silent. In 1901 progressed Jupiter, the "tell it like it is planet" made an exact sextile to his natal Sphinx and closed the trine to natal Jupiter. The Sphinx could no longer remain silent. But, still, Cayce's "trance voice" was gravel-ly and sounded like the voice of someone made of stone. (The Cayce readings revealed the existence of the Dead Sea Scrolls years before they were discovered, almost right under the Sphinx's nose!)

Sisyphus was an entity of ancient times who was required to push a stone ball up the mountain side all day long he dug in and pushed; at night, he rested. But during the night, the stone rolled back down the mountain giving up all, or most, of the ground gained the previous day. Sisyphus represents keeping one's nose to the grindstone, going against the tides, making headway an inch at a time and bearing our crosses. Natal Sisyphus was super-out-of-bounds at 54N56; that requires a major effort. At 10 Leo 59 retrograde, it makes a yod with natal Mercury at 11 Pisces 43 and natal Mars at 11 Capricorn 13, thereby giving him a divine destiny. Edgar Cayce pushed that ball most of his life. He was forced by providence to take up the work ordained for him; he fought against if from day one and finally got out of it by taking up photography, but don't tell us he didn't see a lot more in those pictures than was apparent to the common eye. The placement of Sisyphus in the twelfth house shows his karmic duty to explore the unknown, although he doesn't want to know it (inconjunct Mercury in the angular seventh house) and doesn't want a big deal made out of it (inconjunct Mars in the fifth house). We also see the interaction between him (Sisyphus disposited by the Sun) and his wife (Mercury) and his children (Mars); they all worked together in his endeavors and the children continued the research after his death. In 1901 the solar return Sisyphus at 15 Libra 04 retrograde was in the third house inconjunct natal Venus at 15 Pisces 43 in the eighth house. That year he accepted that he was forced to push the stone, so he might as well make the best of it. Soon afterward, most of his income was derived from the fees of readings performed during Cayce's trances which sapped his energy and taxed vitality. The saving grace was that he knew that his clients were benefitting beyond the scope of standard medical and psychological practice.

The asteroid Atlantis in Edgar Cayce's chart was positioned natally at 21 Capricorn 27 inconjunct his Ascendant and Uranus. Much of his information was gleaned from the psychic recollections of the days when Atlantis was not "The Lost Continent" but was, instead, the most sophisticated place on earth. Atlantis was mentioned so many times in Cayce's later readings that it caught the attention of numerous researchers, both physical and psychic. The result was that by the 1930s people all over the United States were talking about and looking for Atlantis, and they haven't stopped since. Plato mentioned Atlantis but Edgar Cayce made it a household word. Atlantis aspecting both his Ascendant and Uranus and sitting right at his sixth house cusp would indicate that Cayce could well have been personally involved in the health care field during those ancient times.

In 1900, Cayce's progressed Sun in the ninth house at 21 Aries 27 made a square aspect to his natal Atlantis which possibly triggered his conscious memories of that long-ago lifetime. His solar return chart for 1901, the year he actually began his medical readings, had Atlantis at 11 Pisces 31 conjunct his natal Mercury at 11 Pisces 43 and reinforcing the yod between Mercury, Mars and Sisyphus. Many of the objects Cayce described in his Atlantis readings exist today; much of the technology is (re-)emerging today; the attitudes of the Atlanteans that caused their demise are prevalent today. His readings warned us of danger. If Cayce is Sisyphus, then Atlantis is the ball of stone. Can we push it up the hill before it rolls over us, as Cayce suggested that it might?

Finally, Pandora in Edgar Cayce's chart is at 14 Aries 23 and 6N31 contraparallel Venus at 6S56. In 1900, his progressed Venus in the ninth house at 15 Aries 27 opposed natal Pandora. At that point his subconscious opened up and let all, except hope (good karma), fly out and the keys to the future are still in Pandora's box.

Application of Some Selected Asteroids

During 1900-1901, Cayce lost his voice. As a result his health started failing. A doctor who had heard of his health condition came to visit him and suggested that he should be able to hypnotize himself thus be able to perform his own diagnose. The doctor convinced Cayce to examined his own body while in an hypnotic state. As a result Cayce found and administered his cure and upon awakening his voice returned. This event is positively an "I am," Mars situation. Mars was the ruler of his ninth house, his ministry to the world; and in his natal chart was closely sextile, Mercury, Saturn and Venus, trine the Moon and sextile/trine the Nodes.

Note: The error on my part was that I was hesitant to apply Mars to the event and not to worry about Mercury. Mars is the physical strength that must supply the body. Mars had a karmic assignment to perform and he was not, as he would say, "About his Father's (God's) business." What could be more appropriate to Mars than to heal thyself? The energy and power of Pluto in northern declination is sufficient to offset much of the difficulties he faced. He immediately began doing readings.

For more details on using declinations see *Karma by Declinations* by Helen Adams Garrett, and How *Declination Midpoints Expose Details* by Helen Adams Garrett and Rudy Flack. For more information on asteroids see *Asteroid, Mysteries and Messages* by Diane and Rudy Flack.

At age ten, the Moon, which was at 19N58 at birth, progressed into southern declination, bringing Cayce's emotional awareness into karmic play. His Moon was in the power section of declination at birth in Taurus, encouraging him to use his family to assist in the karmic efforts. Cayce was born in one of the long cycles when the Moon went out of bounds every time it progressed to maximum declination, north or south. This is to say, that approximately one fourth of his life the moon was progressed out-of-bounds. What does this mean? It means that he had ability over and beyond what would be expected of him in the area of lunar emotions, lunar productivity and involvement with the general public. The other three-fourths of the world is wondering how on earth people can pay for the enormous homes, mini-castles, that one fourth of the population is buying at the end of the twentieth century? This is because the one-fourth are those with the out-of-bounds moon in most instances and they are doing that which would be beyond what is expected, exercising the ability to pay for it.

Uranus is in northern declination at 15N08 at 21 Leo 15. The energy is in the power section of the declination scale. So we find his power in the ability to be original. Uranus is energized by the square to Pluto and the Moon, which naturally brought some resistance to his originality (Uranus).

Neptune (11N07 and 3 Taurus 39) and Pluto (4N58 and 22 Taurus 55) are both between 0N00 and 14N22 in the talent section. This means that he had talent for application of power from Pluto and with those things represented by Neptune (visions, idealism, compassion, psychic ability).

Chiron is in northern declination at 10N40. This is the talent section of the scale and anyone who pays any attention to Chiron would have to accept the validity of the healer and health advisor for this interpretation. We believe that Chiron also calls for an adjustment of some kind. At birth Chiron was at 27 Aries 58.

Interceptions

The Cayce natal chart has no interceptions. His short ascension houses are first and seventh with twenty-three degrees each. These houses require the least attention from him to run smoothly. This is an applicable statement of a man who slept more than average. The fourth and tenth houses have thirty-four degrees each and require the most attention from him. There is fairly even distribution of degrees among the natal houses thus Cayce did not have to over focus or be forced to deal with intercepted issues via his natal chart.

Although there may not be interceptions in the natal chart this does not rule out such a phenomenon in returns, diurnals, progressions, etc., as used in this study. An interception can occur anywhere in the world at any season, even though there is less of a likelihood at various places and at various times.

Charts included in this study with interceptions are as follows:

1. 1883 solar return: Lost the ability to excerpt knowledge while sleeping with his books under his pillow. Aries and Libra were intercepted in houses 3 and 9. Some communications were closed-out. The duplicated signs were Taurus (Venus) and Scorpio (Pluto). The keys to unlocking the intercepted sign are found in the duplicated sign and are Venus and Pluto which are aspected by the Moon and the Sun. Thus the interceptions would be opened by personal effort.

2. 1900 solar return: Lost his voice. Pisces and Virgo were intercepted in the first and third houses. His personal contacts were limited. The Moon and Saturn ruled the duplicated signs and in difficult positions to activate indicating that the situation would probably prevail through out the year. Voice returned March 31, 1901. His birthday was March 18.

3. March 31, 1901 diurnal: Gemini and Sagittarius are intercepted in the fourth and tenth houses. The closing of that experience put Cayce in action to make a career. Neptune was intercepted in the career house and was the ruler of Pisces, one of the duplicated signs. The ruler of the other duplicated sign was Mercury in the seventh house. He seemed to always have assistance when it was needed.

4. 1903 solar return: Married. Aquarius and Leo were intercepted in houses three and nine. His bride began immediately to be involved in the recording and transcription of his readings. Capricorn and Cancer were the duplicated cusps of those houses. Venus and Pluto, again, are the keys to open the interceptions, this time through communications concerning creativity.

5. 1912 solar return: Wanted to quit. Cayce was not fully aware of the value of his work at the time and he was depleted as a result of negative responses. Aquarius and Leo were intercepted in the first and seventh houses. Gemini and Sagittarius were the duplicated signs on the fifth/sixth and eleventh/twelfth houses. Jupiter and Mercury would be the keys to unlock the restrictions. Indeed it was a doctor who investigated his work and persuaded him to continue.

6. 1925 solar return: Moved to Virginia Beach, Virginia. Virgo and Pisces were intercepted in the sixth and twelfth houses. Interestingly, the purpose and plan was to establish a hospital but many complications arose due to professionalism. The duplicated signs were Cancer, and Capricorn naming Moon and Saturn as the keys to unlock the interception. Sun, Uranus and Venus in the twelfth house intercepted sign kept him in close range all that year doing in house readings.

Conclusion

Most of the major philosophies of the world have been based on what best suits the individual... most people have tended to believe that the soul does not die with the body.

With respect to their beliefs, some people take the preference of a "no return in the physical body" but believe that after death they will continue to live in such a manner so as to spend eternity after death in a spiritual world. Others choose a belief system wherein the soul returns in different bodies at different times thus providing learning experiences allowing them to become more spiritually acceptable with each lifetime. This is referred to as evolving; this repetition of life is referred to as reincarnation (returned in flesh).

Karma could be thought of as a school of discipline in the laws of spiritual development. It is sometimes defined by "cause and effect." Someone else might state this discipline as, "You reap as you sow." Essentially karma infers that whatever occurs in the present comes from issues out of the past.

It is not necessary to believe in reincarnation to accept the philosophy of karma. Many people discover that it may have been easier to accomplish a goal as an adult if they had been more conscientious as a student; that is one-life karma.